50 WALKS IN THE
Lake District

50 Walks in the Lake District

Published by AA Publishing (a trading name of AA Media Limited, whose registered office is Grove House, Lutyens Close, Lychpit, Basingstoke, Hampshire RG24 8AG; registered number 06112600)

© AA Media Limited 2023
Fifth edition
First edition published 2002

Mapping in this book is derived from the following products:
OS Landranger 89 (walks 27, 31-38, 42-46, 49-50)
OS Landranger 90 (walks 3-7, 13-17, 20-23, 29-30)
OS Landranger 96 (walks 11-12, 18-19, 24-26, 39-41, 47-48)
OS Landranger 97 (walks 1-2, 8-10)
OS Explorer 5 (walk 28)

© Crown copyright and database rights 2023 Ordnance Survey. 100021153

Maps contain data available from openstreetmap.org © under the Open Database License found at opendatacommons.org.

ISBN: 978-0-7495-8325-5
ISBN: 978-0-7495-8352-1 (SS)

A CIP catalogue record for this book is available from the British Library.

AA Media would like to thank the following contributors in the preparation of this guide:
Clare Ashton, Tracey Freestone, Lauren Havelock, Nicky Hillenbrand, Ian Little, Richard Marchi, Nigel Phillips and Victoria Samways.

Cover design by berkshire design company.

Printed by Stamperia Artistica Nazionale - Trofarello - TORINO - Italy

A05836

We would like to thank the following photographers, companies and picture libraries for their assistance in the preparation of this book. Abbreviations for the picture credits are as follows:
Alamy = Alamy Stock Photo
Trade cover: PURPLE MARBLES CUMBRIA/Alamy
Special sales cover: Daniel Kay/Alamy
Back cover advert clockwise from bottom left: courtesy of The Plough, Lupton; SolStock/iStock; AA; EmirMemedovski/iStock
Inside: 9 William Collins/Alamy; 12/13 Stuart Little; 29 Ian Goodrick/Alamy; 45 Andrew Craven/Alamy; 55 Andrew Ray/Alamy; 65 Dave Porter/Alamy; 75 Andrew Walmsley/Alamy; 97 greenburn/Alamy; 113 Kumar Sriskandan/Alamy; 129 Stewart Smith/Alamy; 139 Tom Richardson Cumbria/Alamy; 149 Tom Richardson Cumbria/Alamy; 159 William Collins/Alamy; 169 Phil Metcalfe/Alamy

AA

50 WALKS IN THE
Lake District

CONTENTS

How to use this book	6
Exploring the area	8
Walking in safety	10

The walks

WALK		GRADIENT	DISTANCE	PAGE
1	Sedgwick	▲	5.5 miles (8.8km)	14
2	Kendal	▲▲	3 miles (4.8km)	17
3	Wet Sleddale	▲	3.5 miles (5.7km)	20
4	Shap	▲	2.5 miles (4km)	23
5	Penrith	▲	3.8 miles (6.1km)	26
6	Pooley Bridge	▲▲	6 miles (9.7km)	30
7	Kentmere	▲	6.75 miles (10.9km)	33
8	Staveley	▲▲	4 miles (6.4km)	36
9	Cunswick Scar	▲▲	3 miles (4.8km)	39
10	Arnside	▲	5.5 miles (8.8km)	42
11	Grange-over-Sands	▲▲▲	4 miles (6.4km)	46
12	Brant Fell	▲▲	3.5 miles (5.7km)	49
13	Patterdale	▲▲	4 miles (6.4km)	52
14	Aira Force	▲	3 miles (4.8km)	56
15	Caldew	▲	3 miles (4.8km)	59
16	Souther Fell	▲▲▲	5.25 miles (8.4km)	62
17	Ambleside	▲▲▲	3.25 miles (5.3km)	66
18	Satterthwaite	▲▲	4.4 miles (7.15km)	69
19	Grizedale	▲▲	6.4 miles (10.3km)	72
20	Rydal Water	▲	3 miles (4.8km)	76
21	Alcock Tarn	▲▲▲	3 miles (4.8km)	79
22	Elter Water	▲▲	4 miles (6.4km)	82

WALK		GRADIENT	DISTANCE	PAGE
23	Little Langdale	▲	4.5 miles (7.2km)	85
24	Coniston	▲ ▲	6.75 miles (10.9km)	88
25	Swirl How	▲ ▲ ▲	8 miles (12.9km)	91
26	Birkrigg Common	▲ ▲	8.4 miles (13.5km)	94
27	Great Langdale	▲ ▲	2.5 miles (4km)	98
28	St John's in the Vale	▲ ▲ ▲	5 miles (8km)	101
29	Castlerigg	▲	4.1 miles (6.6km)	104
30	Caldbeck	▲ ▲	2 miles (3.2km)	107
31	Keswick	▲ ▲ ▲	5.25 miles (8.4km)	110
32	Cat Bells	▲ ▲ ▲	9 miles (14.5km)	114
33	Binsey	▲ ▲	2.5 miles (4km)	117
34	Bassenthwaite	▲ ▲ ▲	7.5 miles (12.1km)	120
35	Whinlatter	▲ ▲	5 miles (8km)	123
36	Ard Crags	▲ ▲ ▲	5.1 miles (8.2km)	126
37	Stonethwaite	▲ ▲ ▲	5 miles (8km)	130
38	Sty Head	▲ ▲ ▲	5.75 miles (9.2km)	133
39	Seathwaite	▲ ▲	5 miles (8km)	136
40	Broughton-in-Furness	▲ ▲	3.75 miles (6km)	140
41	Duddon Bridge	▲ ▲	6.6 miles (10.5km)	143
42	Eskdale	▲ ▲	6.75 miles (10.9km)	146
43	Buttermere	▲	4.5 miles (7.2km)	150
44	Rannerdale	▲ ▲ ▲	2.9 miles (4.7km)	153
45	Loweswater	▲	5.5 miles (8.8km)	156
46	Nether Wasdale	▲	4.5 miles (7.2km)	160
47	Black Combe	▲ ▲ ▲	8.5 miles (13.7km)	163
48	Muncaster Fell	▲ ▲	6 miles (9.7km)	166
49	Nannycatch Beck	▲ ▲ ▲	9.5 miles (15.3km)	170
50	St Bees Head	▲ ▲	3.25 miles (5.3km)	173

HOW TO USE THIS BOOK

Each walk starts with an information panel giving all the information you will need about the walk at a glance, including its relative difficulty, distance and total amount of ascent. Difficulty levels and gradients are as follows:

Difficulty of walk

● Easy

◐ Intermediate

● Hard

Gradient

▲ Some slopes

▲▲ Some steep slopes

▲▲▲ Several very steep slopes

Maps

Every walk has its own route map. We also suggest a relevant Ordnance Survey map to take with you, allowing you to view the area in more detail. The time suggested is the minimum for reasonably fit walkers and doesn't allow for stops.

Route map legend

_ _ ▶ _ _	Walk route	▢	Built-up area
❶	Route waypoint	▢	Woodland area
_ _ _ _	Adjoining path	🚻	Toilet
●	Place of interest	🅿	Car park
⌂	Steep section	⌸	Picnic area
☀	Viewpoint	)(	Bridge
ⅢⅢⅢⅢ	Embankment		

Start points

The start of each walk is given as a six-figure grid reference prefixed by two letters referring to a 100km square of the National Grid. More information on grid references can be found on most OS Walker's Maps.

Dogs

We have tried to give dog owners useful advice about how dog friendly each walk is. Please respect other countryside users. Keep your dog under control, especially around livestock, and obey local bylaws and other dog control notices.

Car parking

Many of the car parks suggested are public, but occasionally you may have to park on the roadside or in a layby. Please be considerate about where you leave your car, ensuring that you are not on private property or access roads, and that gates are not blocked and other vehicles can pass safely.

Walks locator map

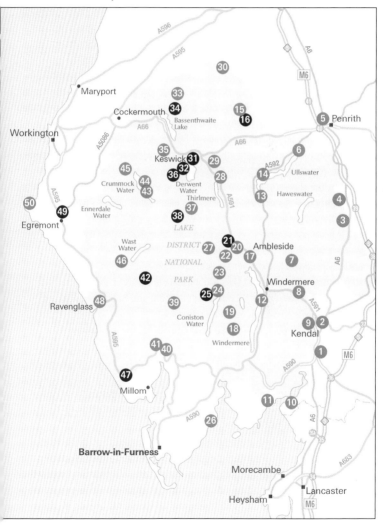

EXPLORING THE AREA

The Lake District occupies a third of Cumbria, one of England's largest counties. At its heart is a series of valleys (dales) cutting through an uplifted button of mountains (fells – the word, like so many here, is Norse in origin). This is a glaciated landscape, where retreating ice more than 15,000 years ago scooped deep hollows that became the lakes we know today. The Lake District National Park Authority oversees 885 square miles (2,292sq km) – England's largest national park – from its headquarters in Kendal.

This is a landscape seemingly made for exploring on foot. When the Romantic poets of the early 19th century began to popularise its picturesque scenery, they did so from its felltops, from its remote daleheads and mountain becks. They took delight in gazing down on the silvery lakes and ever-changing light. So escape the bustle of Bowness with a walk on Brant Fell and see Windermere unfold beneath you, ringed by woodlands. While the crowds gape at Wordsworth's grave in Grasmere, you will be closer to the poet's spirit by the shores of Rydal Water or among the shining tarns and tiny crags of Loughrigg. Keswick sometimes seems like a retail park, so why not rise above the mêlée and look down from Walla Crag, Cat Bells or Latrigg.

There's grand isolation too, on the rounded, grassy northern fells above Bassenthwaite and Mungrisedale. Breathtaking sights await in the central Lakes, where you'll find quiet sides to Coniston and Langdale. Quieter all round are the western Lakes. Dunnerdale is barely changed since Wordsworth's day. Remote Eskdale will enchant and Nannycatch delight even those who think they know this area well.

But there is more to the Lake District than just the area within the National Park boundary. To the south, vast Morecambe Bay is fringed by delightful limestone outcrops. To the northeast and far west, red sandstone rises from the green farmland. In the east, Penrith Beacon looks out over the Vale of Eden stretching north to the Scottish border, and to the formidable Lakeland skyline. To the far west, the cliffs of St Bees look out over the restless Irish Sea.

The big fells draw hundreds of thousands of walkers and climbers to the heart of the Lake District National Park, but there is plenty of space, and a few minutes after escaping from your car, you will often find yourself alone in breathtaking countryside. You may spot elusive wildlife on your way, like osprey, red deer and red squirrels; the distinctive fell breeds of sheep – Rough Fell, Herdwick, Swaledale – are still familiar companions as well. The Lakeland landscape is as varied on these walks as many counties can claim in their entirety. So whether you're drawn by the literary connections, the breathtaking views, the quiet wooded corners or the majesty of lonely fellsides, you will not be disappointed.

In December 2015, Storm Desmond hit the UK and its devastating effects centred on Cumbria. Homes and livelihoods were destroyed, along with nearly 800 bridges. The community has worked hard to get back on its feet, but you may still see the odd sign of the damage done.

PUBLIC TRANSPORT

The Lake District is fairly well served by public transport. The railway to Windermere and the bus service onward to Ambleside, Grasmere and Keswick, are the backbone of the network. Boat services on four lakes, and even steam trains, are useful as well as fun, but local bus services are key. However, some services are seasonal and only a few run on into the evenings, so plan carefully: visit www.visitlakedistrict.com/explore/travel.

Walk 45

WALKING IN SAFETY

All these walks are suitable for any reasonably fit person, but less experienced walkers should try the easier walks first. Route-finding is usually straightforward, but you will find that an Ordnance Survey walking map is a useful addition to the route maps and descriptions; recommendations can be found in the information panels.

Risks

Although each walk here has been researched with a view to minimising the risks to the walkers who follow its route, no walk in the countryside can be considered to be completely free from risk. Walking in the outdoors will always require a degree of common sense and judgement to ensure that it is as safe as possible.

- Be particularly careful on cliff paths and in upland terrain, where the consequences of a slip can be very serious.

- Remember to check tidal conditions before walking on the seashore.

- Some sections of route are by, or cross, busy roads. Take care, and remember that traffic is a danger even on minor country lanes.

- Be careful around farmyard machinery and livestock, especially if you have children with you.

- Be aware of the consequences of changes in the weather, and check the forecast before you set out. Carry spare clothing and a torch if you are walking in the winter months. Remember that the weather can change very quickly at any time of the year, and in moorland and heathland areas, mist and fog can make route-finding much harder. Don't set out in these conditions unless you are confident of your navigation skills in poor visibility.

- In summer remember to take account of the heat and sun; wear a hat and carry sufficient water.

- On walks away from centres of population you should carry a whistle and survival bag. If you do have an accident that means you require help from the emergency services, make a note of your position as accurately as possible and dial 999.

Countryside Code
Respect other people:

- Consider the local community and other people enjoying the outdoors.

- Co-operate with people at work in the countryside. For example, keep out of the way when farm animals are being gathered or moved, and follow directions from the farmer.

- Don't block gateways, driveways or other paths with your vehicle.
- Leave gates and property as you find them, and follow paths unless wider access is available, such as on open country or registered common land (known as 'open access land').
- Leave machinery and farm animals alone – don't interfere with animals, even if you think they're in distress. Try to alert the farmer instead.
- Use gates, stiles or gaps in field boundaries if you can – climbing over walls, hedges and fences can damage them and increase the risk of farm animals escaping.
- Our heritage matters to all of us – be careful not to disturb ruins and historic sites.

Protect the natural environment:
- Take your litter home. Litter and leftover food don't just spoil the beauty of the countryside; they can be dangerous to wildlife and farm animals. Dropping litter and dumping rubbish are criminal offences.
- Leave no trace of your visit, and take special care not to damage, destroy or remove features such as rocks, plants and trees.
- Keep dogs under effective control, making sure they are not a danger or nuisance to farm animals, horses, wildlife or other people.
- If cattle or horses chase you and your dog, it is safer to let your dog off the lead – don't risk getting hurt by trying to protect it. Your dog will be much safer if you let it run away from a farm animal in these circumstances, and so will you.
- Everyone knows how unpleasant dog mess is and it can cause infections, so always clean up after your dog and get rid of the mess responsibly – bag it and bin it.
- Fires can be as devastating to wildlife and habitats as they are to people and property – so be careful with naked flames and cigarettes at any time of the year.

Enjoy the outdoors:
- Plan ahead and be prepared for natural hazards, changes in weather and other events.
- Wild animals, farm animals and horses can behave unpredictably if you get too close, especially if they're with their young – so give them plenty of space.
- Follow advice and local signs.

For more information visit www.gov.uk/government/publications/the-countryside-code

SEDGWICK AND THE LANCASTER CANAL

DISTANCE/TIME	5.5 miles (8.8km) / 2hrs 30min
ASCENT/GRADIENT	600ft (183m) / ▲
PATHS	Field paths, tow paths and some quiet lanes, many stiles
LANDSCAPE	Grazing fields cover rolling landscape, distant hills
SUGGESTED MAP	OS Explorer OL7 The English Lakes (SE)
START/FINISH	Grid reference: SD513870
DOG FRIENDLINESS	On lead along lanes and where livestock are grazing
PARKING	Roadside parking in Sedgwick
PUBLIC TOILETS	None on route

The 18th century saw the beginnings of industrialisation in Britain, when machines were invented that performed the labour of umpteen people. Nowhere was the transformation more startling than in the textile industries, where large, water-powered mills replaced an age-old tradition of home working. Mechanisation affected other areas too, but the limiting factor to expansion was transport. Factories located beside navigable water could trade by boat, but the fast-flowing rivers and streams powering the new machinery lay far inland, accessible only by packhorses or lumbering carts. A second revolution came with the development of canals, which effectively took the seaboard into the heart of the countryside. Now serviced by cheap and speedy transport, the areas they reached profited from burgeoning new industries.

A new age

Kendal had long been a successful town, flourishing from the woollen and other industries, but remoteness from the main population and industrial centres became an increasing threat to prosperity. So, in 1792, a waterway linking Kendal to the industrial heartland of Lancashire via Lancaster and Preston was sanctioned. By 1797 barges were passing between Tewitfield and Preston. The final section was this stretch into Kendal, routed via Sedgwick to take in the gunpowder factories beside the River Kent, which served the many limestone quarries in the area. However, blocking the way was a hill, and the only means of avoiding a lengthy detour was to burrow straight through. Completed in 1817, the Hincaster Tunnel is 378yds (346m) long and, as you will see, remains a magnificent feat of engineering. To minimise expense, the tunnel did not include a tow path; barges were pulled through by hand using a fixed cable, or 'legged' by the bargees. Further obstacles lay in river and other crossings, two of which are passed on this ramble.

Although the aqueduct across Stainton Beck is hardly apparent from above, it is also a notable achievement. So is the skew aqueduct at Sedgwick, where the walk begins. Have a look at its stonework as you pass beneath. A traditional arch would have had to extend over the full width of the crossing to retain its inherent strength. But, by laying the courses at an angle, the integrity of the structure was retained, allowing the span to be matched to the crossing. Commercial traffic ended in 1947, and the northern stretch was drained in 1955, with more sections disappearing beneath the M6 motorway and Kendal bypass. However, what remains is full of interest and a delight to explore.

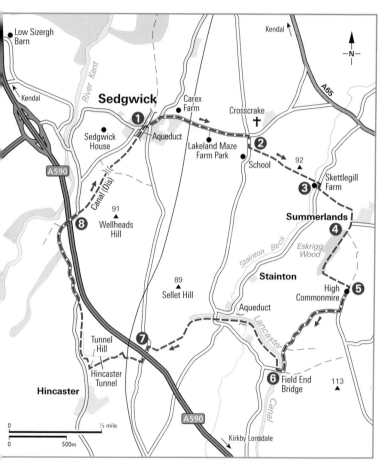

1. From the canal aqueduct, walk gently uphill as far as the second junction by Carex Farm and turn right. Just before Crosscrake church go right again, signed 'Stainton Cross'.

2. Leave through the first gate on the left, and cross to a stile in the far right corner of the field. Follow the left-hand hedge to a second stile. Beyond the crest, drop to cross Stainton Beck by a farm, then exit to a lane.

3. From the gate opposite go up to another gate. Continue in the same direction across the next field, passing a waymark, to a stile in the corner.

Walk to the far wall and turn right along it. Cross a stile to a track and continue in the same direction, slightly downhill.

4. Walk down the track, passing through a gate by Eskrigg Wood. The way shortly broadens into a meadow, but keep going to the further of two gates at the left corner. A waymark confirms the route along a hedged track into rough woodland. Soon the path bends left to a stile. Walk straight up a field to a gate left of a tree.

5. Turn right along a track leading through a small, gated farmyard at High Commonmire, and continuing beyond as a tarmac byway. Turn right at a junction and carry on down to the canal and a bridge.

6. Cross the canal, drop left onto the tow path and walk beneath the bridge. Cross an aqueduct over Stainton Beck. A section beyond this is currently being restored, but the canal's course is always clear. Follow it, eventually coming to a lane below the A590.

7. Pass under the bridge and rejoin the canal through a gate on the right. A cutting leads to the mouth of the Hincaster Tunnel, where a path to the left carries walkers, as it once did horses, over Tunnel Hill. At the far side, turn right beside a house to regain the tow path. Remain by the canal until forced onto the lane and continue eventually to cross the A590.

8. Just beyond the bridge, steps rise to a field on the right. Go up and then left along the wire fence, and on across the field, eventually passing beneath a lone bridge. Beyond, the canal cutting is again evident, accompanying you back to Sedgwick and the start of the walk, where steps beside the aqueduct drop to the road.

Where to eat and drink
Surprisingly, there are no inns or tea rooms at Sedgwick, but a visit to nearby Low Sizergh Barn Café, where you can have a light lunch or snack, is heartily recommended. If you pick the right time, you can even watch the cows being milked while you eat.

What to see
The area crossed by this walk is part of a notable drumlin field. Drumlins are low hills, often streamlined in appearance, created by ice sheets smoothing out the debris they had deposited. The hill you cross after Point 2 and Tunnel Hill are both good examples. You may be able to see why this kind of landscape is sometimes called a 'basket of eggs'.

While you're there
Nearby Levens Hall (to the west, just off the A6) is a real gem. Surrounded by a fantastic topiary garden, the splendid Elizabethan house was built around a 14th-century pele tower, constructed by the de Redman family. Later owners transformed its spartan chambers into a comfortable country residence. Beautifully maintained, it contains a host of treasures, including exquisite wood panelling, carvings and plaster mouldings.

2

KENDAL'S TWO CASTLES

DISTANCE/TIME	3 miles (4.8km) / 1hr 30min
ASCENT/GRADIENT	300ft (91m) / ▲ ▲
PATHS	Pavements, surfaced and grassy paths with steps
LANDSCAPE	Historic townscape and parkland
SUGGESTED MAP	OS Explorer OL7 The English Lakes (SE)
START/FINISH	Grid reference: SD516925
DOG FRIENDLINESS	Parkland is popular with dog walkers, but busy roads through town
PARKING	Westmorland Shopping Centre car park, above Kendal bus station
PUBLIC TOILETS	In Westmorland Shopping Centre

Known as the 'Auld Grey Town', because of the colour of its predominantly limestone buildings, enterprising Kendal retains much of its original character. Until 1974 this was the administrative centre for the former county of Westmorland. Sited either side of the River Kent, its occupation stretches from Roman times to the present day and its varied stone buildings, nooks, crannies, yards and castles offer a rich historical tapestry. This walk visits two important strongholds located strategically on high ground either side of the river: Kendal Castle and Castle Howe.

Kendal Castle

Sited in a commanding position above the town and the River Kent, ruined Kendal Castle is quietly impressive and offers fine views in all directions. Kendal people may tell you that this was the birthplace of Catherine Parr, who became Henry VIII's sixth and last wife in 1543. Although her grandfather, William Parr (d.1483), lies entombed in Kendal parish church, there is no clear evidence that Catherine ever set foot in Kendal, and the castle was probably already falling into decay by that time.

It is thought that Kendal Castle succeeded Castle Howe, sited on the opposite side of the river, sometime in the late 12th century. After the Norman barons had secured the kingdom; they required quarters with sufficient space to administer their feudal territories and so replaced their wooden motte and bailey castles with castles of stone. This happened here about 1220, with the construction of Kendal Castle starting while the motte and bailey Castle Howe was still in use. Work continued until 1280 by one of the early barons of Kendal, either Gilbert Fitzreinfrid or his son William de Lancaster. Today the ruins of Kendal Castle consist of a circular defensive wall and three towers plus a residential gatehouse surrounded by a partly filled ditch. The entrance path leads through the wall at the point where a gatehouse once stood. To the left are the largest standing remains, the house where the baron's family lived, known as the Lyons Den, or Machell Tower. To the right stands the Northwest

Tower, with a 'dungeon room' below, and garderobe (toilet), with free fall into the ditch/moat, above. Substantial new steps now lead up the tower, and another set allows you to view the 'Manor House', which was the main living quarters of the castle. The Parr family occupied the castle for four generations, from 1380 to 1486, when William Parr's widow remarried and moved to Northamptonshire. The castle fell into ruin and much of the stone is thought to have been recycled for use in building works in the town below.

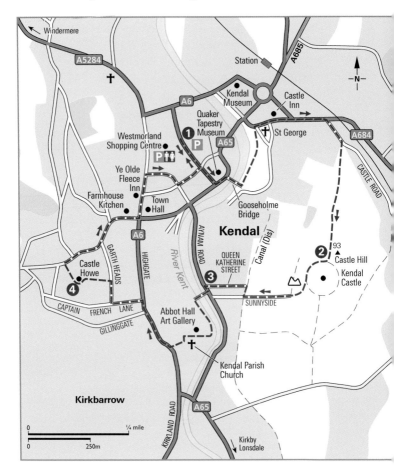

1. From the car park exit (Level 1) by the bus station, turn right down Blackhall Road to a pedestrian crossing near the river. Cross, then turn left to a footbridge. Cross, and turn left to follow the surfaced walkway through Gooseholme. At the road junction beyond the Church of St George, turn right down Castle Street. Pass the Castle Inn and continue up the hill to Castle Road on the right. Ascend Castle Road and go through a kissing gate on the right onto Castle Hill. Follow the broad path up the hill to the Kendal Castle ruins.

2. Go round the right (west) side of the castle ruins and soon fork right. Descend steeply to an iron kissing gate, and join a street. Go over a bridge,

then drop down right, to the course of the old canal. Walk away from the bridge, and in a few paces turn left into a quiet street.

3. At the end go left a few paces to a crossing and a footbridge over the River Kent. Over the river turn left, downstream, and just before reaching the parish church turn right to pass between the church and Abbot Hall Art Gallery on a path lined with yew trees. Bear slightly left to emerge onto busy Kirkland Road by the impressive iron gates of the church. Turn right along the road to a crossing. Cross it, then turn right to cross Gillinggate and keep along the main road, now called Highgate. Take the next left up Captain French Lane for 300yds (274m), then turn right up Garth Heads. Follow this until steep steps ascend to the left. Climb to a terrace and a view out over Kendal. Cross the grass terrace towards the mound and its distinct bodkin-shaped obelisk. Climb the steps then spiral left. As the path levels, steps lead up right to the obelisk and the top of Castle Howe.

4. Return to the path and go right. Find a gap on the left and emerge on the road at the top of a steep hill. Descend the hill, which becomes Allhallows Lane, to the traffic lights and pedestrian crossing opposite the Town Hall. Turn left, escaping the traffic, along Stricklandgate. Take the second right down Market Place. The easiest way now is through the Westmorland Shopping Centre, but a more characterful route is to continue down the steep hill. Turn left on Stramongate and left again to return to the start.

Where to eat and drink

Kendal is famed for its many fine pubs, cafés and restaurants. The Farmhouse Kitchen (fhk), near the bottom of Allhallows Lane, is excellent. Just round the corner, Ye Olde Fleece Inn dates to 1654.

What to see

Castle Howe, Kendal's first Norman motte and bailey castle, was built between 1068 and 1100, but all that remains of it now is the 36ft-high (11m) motte (mound). Located at the northern edge of the rapidly established Norman kingdom, the town, then known as Kirkbie Strickland, was mentioned in the Domesday survey of 1086. The obelisk on top of the motte was designed by Francis Webster and built by William Holme in 1788 to mark the centenary of the Glorious Revolution of 1688, when William of Orange replaced James II. It is known locally as 'Bill Holmes' Bodkin'.

While you're there

There are many things to see in this historic town. Kendal Museum has everything from stuffed bears and crocodiles to neolithic Langdale stone axes. The town's finest historic home, 18th-century Abbot Hall, is an art gallery, staging exhibitions of international artists. 'Parish church' suggests a much more humble building than the impressive Grade I listed Kendal parish church, with its soaring, airy interior and 800-year-old nave. The Quaker Tapestry Museum in town tells the story of the Society of Friends through a series of embroidered panels.

WITHNAIL AND WET SLEDDALE

DISTANCE/TIME	3.5 miles (5.7km) / 1hr 30min
ASCENT/GRADIENT	262ft (80m) / ▲
PATHS	Boggy field paths, track and lane, 1 stile
LANDSCAPE	Wet upland pasture and reservoir
SUGGESTED MAP	OS Explorer OL5 The English Lakes (NE)
START/FINISH	Grid reference: NY554114
DOG FRIENDLINESS	Fields grazed by sheep, so dogs must be under close control; signs request that in spring and summer dogs are kept on leads because of ground-nesting birds
PARKING	Car park by Wet Sleddale dam
PUBLIC TOILETS	None on route

'We've gone on holiday by mistake. We're in this cottage here. Are you the farmer?'
Withnail, *Withnail and I* (1986)

In 1985 filmmaker Bruce Robinson chose Sleddale Hall as a location for his 1960s-based tale of two unemployed actors, *Withnail and I*, and this quiet valley on the eastern fringe of the Lake District has never been the same since. Telling the semi-autobiographical story of Marwood ('I', played by Paul McGann) and his exploits with the debauched Withnail (Richard E Grant), the film follows the London-based thespians as they embark on a holiday in the Lake District. Withnail's Uncle Monty (played by Richard Griffiths and who Robinson has suggested was inspired by his encounters in 1968 with Italian director Franco Zefferelli) owns a tumbledown farmhouse in the hills – Cow Crag in the film, but Sleddale Hall in reality – that they attempt to use as a holiday cottage. The hall, originally a deserted hill farm, was transformed with minimal set building into the grim northern wilds of Withnail's imagination.

Other locations nearby include the packhorse bridge where Marwood and Withnail attempt to catch fish with a shotgun (crossed in this walk), and the phone box in Bampton, where Withnail tries to talk to his agent. Somewhat mundanely the 'Penrith Tearooms' and pub scenes were shot near Milton Keynes, and the 'view' from Cow Crag is of neighbouring Haweswater, not Sleddale's diminutive reservoir.

Ironically the film made little money on its initial release, scant reward for the late George Harrison, the ex-Beatle whose Handmade Films had stumped up half the £1.1 million it took to make. Grant went on to become a Hollywood star, and McGann became Dr Who. When United Utilities put the house up for sale in 2009 it was bought by a fan for over £250,000. It is on private property and is not open to the public.

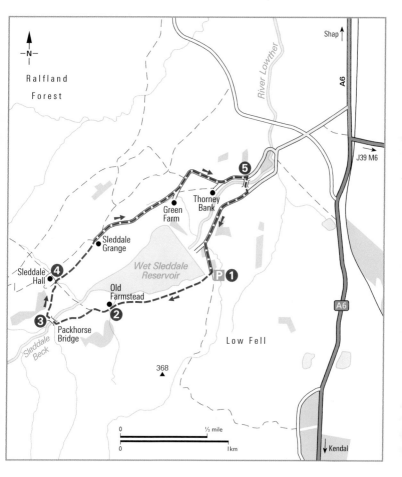

1. Leave the car park by the dam at its far end, walking up a damp track towards a gate by a clump of trees. Beyond the gate follow the boggy track up the valley, ignoring a turning to the left.

2. The track peters out by an old farmstead near the head of the reservoir. Maintain your direction, through one gate, over a little footbridge and through a second gate. Skirt round the edge of a boggy area before picking up a clearer track again through a gap in a wall. The path continues to be damp until you reach a stone bridge over Sleddale Beck on the right.

3. Cross the bridge and climb the bank on the far side to a stile. Turn right along the ascending track. Beyond a copse of trees there is a junction by a barn. Sleddale Hall is directly up the slope above you and you can walk around its perimeter, returning to this point. Remember the hall is private property and there is no public access to the building itself.

4. Go through the gate beside the barn and walk along a farm track, now heading back out of the valley. Approaching the farm buildings at Sleddale Grange, go through a gate and thread between a shed and some sheep pens to another gate, emerging on the far side and finally leaving the farm buildings by

a gate onto a surfaced road. Follow the descending road for a mile (1.6km), passing through a gate by Green Farm and continuing on through yet another gate down to Thorney Bank.

5. A few hundred yards beyond this farm, a narrow path drops down to the right and through a gate to a footbridge. Cross the bridge and, on the far side, join the surfaced road, turning right to walk back up to the car park by the dam.

Where to eat and drink

Instead of turning left back into Shap, turn right and shortly you'll see a sign for the Shap Wells Hotel. Hidden away at the foot of a winding moorland road, this venerable hotel has been serving travellers for centuries and is still a splendid spot for a good lunch or dinner. There's a bar serving local ales too.

What to see

The packhorse bridge crossed at the mid-way point of this walk feels genuine enough, and indeed its materials are. The whole structure, however, used to be half a mile or so (800m) downstream, in a position now under the reservoir. It was relocated to its current position when the dam was built in the 1960s.

While you're there

Shap Abbey, on the other side of the one-street town, is worth a visit. Founded by a reclusive order of Premonstratensian canons in the 13th century, the most impressive feature is the West Tower, added barely 40 years before the abbey's dissolution in 1540.

SHAP ABBEY AND ROSGILL

DISTANCE/TIME	2.5 miles (4km) / 1hr 30min
ASCENT/GRADIENT	885ft (270m) / ▲
PATHS	Mostly grassy paths and tracks, 7 stiles
LANDSCAPE	Fields and valley
SUGGESTED MAP	OS Explorer OL5 The English Lakes (NE)
START/FINISH	Grid reference: NY547153
DOG FRIENDLINESS	Most fields grazed by sheep, so care must be exercised
PARKING	Parking area at Shap Abbey; follow signs from A6 in Shap village
PUBLIC TOILETS	None on route

The Premonstratensians came to 'Hepp' (meaning 'heap') in 1199, from a site near Kendal at Preston Patrick. They craved solitude and austerity, and by the banks of the River Lowther they found both. The white-coated canons (they weren't actually monks) set about building a church and developing the land around them to supply food and a trading surplus to fund their work. This was never a huge place – there would have been an abbot and only 12 canons, with perhaps a handful of lay brothers to act as servants. By comparison, the Cistercian house at Fountains in Yorkshire, which acquired significant landholdings throughout the Dales and Lake District, numbered as many as 52 monks and a veritable army of retainers.

Main building and tower
The abbey building was founded with money from local noble families, and originally had a cross-shaped plan, with a range of outbuildings you can still discern today. In the 15th century the nave was extended and there was an attempt to put up a grand tower over the crossing. There were structural problems, however, and the idea was abandoned. It wasn't until 1500 that the plans were revived. Under the instruction of the ambitious abbot Richard Redman (who went on to become Bishop of Ely), the masons who had recently worked on the impressive new towers at Furness and Fountains were engaged to deliver a similar product at Shap. Taking heed of lessons learned, they shunned the unstable crossing and built at the west end instead. The tower, in the typical Perpendicular style of the day, still stands pretty much at its original height.

Dissolution and beyond
Ironically the foundation it served was to last barely 40 more years. In 1540 the last abbot was pensioned off on £40 per year and became the vicar at Kirkby Thore near Penrith. Henry VIII's administrators moved in and sold the estates to Sir Thomas Wharton, the governor of Carlisle. In the 18th century they came

to the Lowther family and in 1896 the Earl of Lonsdale removed most of the good remaining carved stonework to decorate his garden at Lowther Park in anticipation of a visit that year from the German Kaiser. The ruins have been cared for by the state since 1948.

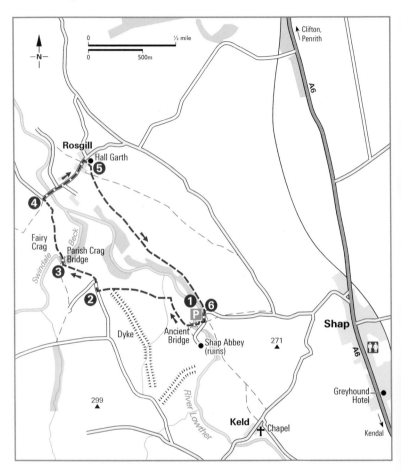

1. From the little car park, walk over the ancient bridge and through the wider of the two gates on the other side. To visit the abbey ruins, keep straight on here, making for the entrance beneath the tower. Otherwise turn immediately right, up the bank to a gate and follow the riverside path beyond, rounding the river bend before striking off left across the field. A faint field path heads for a gate in the wall ahead. As you go through this you'll see the ongoing route, down into a dip then over a shoulder. Beyond the brow, keep to the right of the wall. As it bends left, maintain your direction to reach a stile. Cross and continue on a faint field path to a stile beside a gate. Cross this to reach a surfaced farm track.

2. Turn right, then as the path bends left, leave it for a small gate beside some tumbledown farm buildings on the right. On the far side of the old farmyard a stone stile leads through the wall. Head half left down the field towards a fence corner. Some steps lead to the gate at Parish Crag Bridge.

3. Cross the ancient packhorse bridge and on the other side bear right, following the fence around the outcrop of Fairy Crag. Soon you have a wall on your right, and beyond that you go over a high wall topped by a gate. Stay with the wall at the foot of a bank, soon to reach a pair of gates. Walk along the farm track beyond, which meets a road by a bridge.

4. Turn right, go over the bridge and up into Rosgill. Ascending the street, look for an opening on the right between Fell View and Hall Garth.

5. Squeeze through a stile and gate and another gate, then walk across the short field to another stile. Cross the middle of a narrow field to a gate. Take the right-hand option of two footpath arrows, and stay on this level field path. There are two gates on the far side of the field. Go through the one on the left. Pass a farm building and, staying on the level route, go through the left-hand wooden gate. A wall joins you briefly on the right, but it is soon lost again as your route follows the bank top through several more gates. Finally a ladder stile keeps you to the left of an old farm, and you emerge on the concrete access road to the abbey.

6. Turn right and walk down the hill to return to the car park.

Where to eat and drink

Shap has a range of pubs and cafés, especially popular with walkers on the Coast to Coast route. The biggest is probably the Greyhound Hotel, a former coaching inn, which serves food in both its bar and restaurant and boasts a large range of real ales.

What to see

The first section of this route, from the abbey to the road at Rosgill, is coincidental with the famous Coast to Coast Walk. Devised by the late Alfred Wainwright, it's a 190-mile trail (305km) from St Bees on Cumbria's Irish Sea coast all the way across the Lakes, Pennines and North York Moors to finish at Robin Hood's Bay on the shores of the North Sea.

While you're there

Shap is a peculiar mix of roadside industrial village and ancient settlement site. As well as some interesting standing stones littered about the area, there is a tiny 15th-century chapel in the hamlet of Keld, barely a mile (1.6km) from the abbey. It's cared for by the National Trust and there are instructions on how to obtain a key on the door if you want to look inside.

ON PENRITH BEACON

DISTANCE/TIME	3.8 miles (6.1km) / 1hr 45min
ASCENT/GRADIENT	560ft (171m) / ▲
PATHS	Good paths and pavements
LANDSCAPE	Town and woodland
SUGGESTED MAP	OS Explorer OL5 The English Lakes (NE)
START/FINISH	Grid reference: NY516303
DOG FRIENDLINESS	Can be off lead on Beacon Hill but not elsewhere
PARKING	Car park at Penrith bus station
PUBLIC TOILETS	At bus station

Beacons were once a means of communication; great fires lit on prominent hills would warn the surrounding community and watchers on far-off hillsides of approaching danger. In the days before the telegraph this was typically the fastest way of spreading news. Penrith's Beacon has a direct line of sight with Orton Scar to the south, and Carlisle Castle about 18 miles (29km) to the north. Here, the danger that required such warnings was usually a raid by the Scots: they ransacked Penrith on several occasions, the last being in 1745.

The Old Pretender
In an attempt to restore James Stuart (1688–1766), the 'Old Pretender', to the throne as James III, the Jacobites rose in 1715 and marched south with an army of Highlanders. Joined by the Earl of Derwentwater and 'a parcel of north country jockeys and foxhunters' at Brampton, they advanced on Penrith. Beacons were lit and the Cumberland and Westmorland militia called out. Accompanied by several thousand yeomen, farmers and labourers, they marched to intercept the Jacobite forces at Penrith Fell. However, when they encountered the advance guard, the defending army ran away, leaving their commanders, Lord Lonsdale and Bishop Nicholson, to fend for themselves. Lonsdale fled to Appleby, and the bishop's coachman drove his master home to Rose Castle. The Jacobites levied a contribution of £500 on Penrith but otherwise left it undisturbed. The rebellion ended in failure and Derwentwater had his estates forfeited and his head chopped off.

The Young Pretender
Following the defeat of the 1715 rebellion Penrith enjoyed 30 years of relative peace. Then the Jacobites struck again; this time at their head came James's son, Prince Charles Edward (1720–88), the 'Young Pretender' or 'Bonnie Prince Charlie'. He marched south with an army of Highlanders, taking Carlisle, and in November 1745 arrived in Penrith, where he met no opposition. The rebel army subsequently got as far as Derby, but indecisiveness delayed them and eventually they turned back. Penrith Beacon was lit again to call the countryside to arms. News that the Jacobites were in retreat encouraged people to turn out to cut off the stragglers. On 15 December, at Langwathby,

a Penrith party defeated 110 of the Jacobites' Hussars but later that day Highland troops, under Lord George Murray, defeated a Hanoverian force at Clifton Moor. Murray joined the Prince at Penrith, ready to leave for the long march north and eventual defeat at Culloden Moor.

The red sandstone tower on the Beacon summit was built in 1719 and restored in 1780. It's thought that the last time the Beacon was lit for warning purposes was during the Napoleonic wars in the early 19th century.

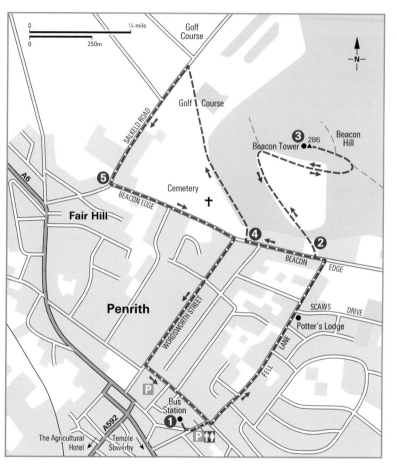

1. From the bus station car park, exit to Sandgate and turn left. Go right and left at a double mini-roundabout and ascend Fell Lane to Beacon Edge. Go left a short way, then right up a path signed 'Permitted Footpath Beacon Summit'.

2. Follow the fenced path up through the trees, soon swinging left. Higher up there's a short section over exposed sandstone bedrock. Shortly after this the path swings back right. The fence on the left ends, but the one on the right continues, apart from a short break. The main path is never in doubt. The path bends left, levels out, then turns sharp left again, leading to the Beacon tower now visible ahead.

3. From the top of Beacon Hill, with its views into the Lake District, retrace your route to Beacon Edge. Turn right and follow the road to a path signed to Salkeld Road.

4. Turn right and follow the path along the back of the town cemetery. Nearing a bench beyond the cemetery, ignore the clear path veering right with the wall up into the woods; instead, pass directly behind the bench and through a gate to arrive at a golf course. Cross the fairways with due caution, following frequent waymarks, to reach a small, red, stone building. There's a squeeze stile to the left of the building. Go through this and turn left down Salkeld Road. There's an even wider view of the Lakeland skyline from here than from the Beacon summit. Turn left down Salkeld Road.

5. At the junction with Beacon Edge, turn left and walk past the front of the cemetery. Almost opposite its end, turn right and go down Wordsworth Street. At the bottom of the hill, at a mini-roundabout, turn left. Walk along here, passing the Quaker Meeting House and soon reaching the double mini-roundabout of the outward journey. Turn right, back into Sandgate, and right again to re-enter the bus station car park.

Where to eat and drink
The Agricultural Hotel in Castlegate, next to Morrison's supermarket, is one of the great pubs of Cumbria. Warm and friendly, it serves a wide variety of pub grub including local specialities such as black pudding. You can wash it all down with a pint of Jennings ale.

What to see
Penrith has many wonderful and unusual buildings. Sandgate Hall is a 17th-century town house, unaltered since it was built apart from the modern windows. Potter's Lodge, on the corner of Fell Lane and Scaws Drive, is a fine example of Georgian architecture.

While you're there
Acorn Bank Garden and Watermill is a National Trust property at Temple Sowerby. The garden is protected by oak trees, and you can walk through the orchards and by the mixed borders. It has the largest collection of herbs in the North and there's a woodland walk leading to the watermill.

ANCIENT SITES ABOVE POOLEY BRIDGE

DISTANCE/TIME	6 miles (9.7km) / 3hrs
ASCENT/GRADIENT	1,130ft (345m) / ▲ ▲
PATHS	Surfaced roads, stony tracks, grassy tracks, open hillside and woodland trails
LANDSCAPE	Village, dale, open fell and woodland
SUGGESTED MAP	OS Explorer OL5 The English Lakes (NE)
START/FINISH	Grid reference: NY469245
DOG FRIENDLINESS	Under strict control as sheep and ponies roam open fell
PARKING	Dunmallard car park on western edge of Pooley Bridge
PUBLIC TOILETS	Pooley Bridge village centre

This figure-of-eight walk first climbs a small hill topped by an Iron Age hill-fort before heading on to the open, grassy fellside above Pooley Bridge. It offers extensive views west over Ullswater, north across the stone buildings of Pooley Bridge and east to the Eden Valley and the hills of the North Pennines. Ancient look-out Dunmallard Hill, sometimes known as Dunmallet, is topped by the earthwork remains of an Iron Age fort. Commanding a striking defensive site above the river crossing at Pooley Bridge, 2,000 years ago it would have been part of the territory of the Brigantes, a Celtic tribe who controlled much of what is now northern England.

Antiquities of Moor Divock

Ancient relics of prehistory, scattered across the high ground of Moor Divock, add an air of mystery and intrigue to this outing. The short section of the High Street Roman road followed on this walk leads directly to the Cockpit stone circle. This is distinct and unmistakable and, as it is thought to be of Bronze Age origin (c.2000 BC), it predates the Roman road. Two concentric circles of stones, some standing, some fallen, contain a stone and earth circular bank up to 3ft (1m) high. It has an internal radius of around 85ft (26m). In more recent times it was probably used for cockfighting, which was outlawed in 1849.

Extending southeast from here is desolate Moor Divock where, hidden amongst the stark landscape of coarse hill grass, bracken, heather and bog, are many prehistoric burial mounds and cairns. A mound known as White Raise, presumably because of the white quartz which marks its rocks, when partially excavated in the 19th century revealed a crouched skeleton in one of its cists (a coffin or burial chamber of stone or wood). Nearby, the Cop Stone is a standing stone some 5ft (1.6m) high. Local sports were held by this stone until 1800, and tradition claims that an avenue of standing stones once led to it. Two further Bronze Age stone circles close by, referred to as Moor Divock 4 and Moor Divock 5, have been partially excavated to reveal urns and ashes.

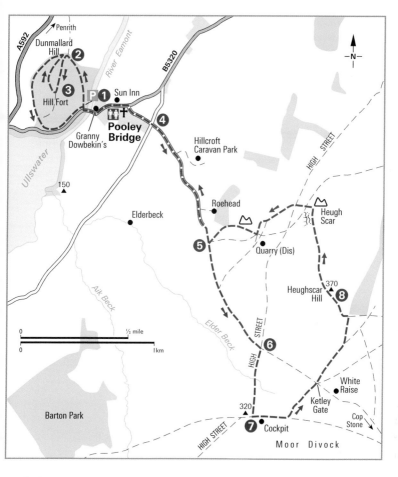

1. From the car park entrance, go through the gate on the right and then immediately bear right to follow the ascending path.

2. Where a public footpath signed 'Dacre' cuts off down to the right, a worn muddy path climbs the bank to the left. This path leads steeply up the wooded slopes of Dunmallard Hill before levelling off slightly. A final section of steep bank leads over the earth ramparts of the fort and onto the tree-clad summit area. Nearing the highest point, keep left at a fork. Gaps in the foliage show how impressive a viewpoint this would be if the trees were thinned.

3. Return to the fork just encountered and descend left. Watch carefully for the next split in the path, where you should turn right. Join the footpath near the base of the hill just beyond Point 2 and go left, following the path around the hill anticlockwise. This eventually leads back to the gate at the entrance to the car park at Point 1. Cross over the River Eamont on the B5320 to enter the village of Pooley Bridge. Continue through the village and then turn right after the church, along High Street.

4. At the junction continue over the crossroads. The road rises and becomes tree-lined before ending at an unsurfaced track. Gates lead onto the moor.

5. Go through one of the gates and climb the wide track, continuing to where the path levels at a fingerpost and another track crosses. (This is the third, and most obvious, path crossing since leaving the road.)

6. Turn right along the stony path – the route of the High Street Roman road. Just before it bends right, there is a low, circular, ancient wall of earth and stone on the left. This is the Cockpit, the largest of the prehistoric antiquities on Moor Divock.

7. Take the path, indistinct at first, left of the Cockpit. This swings left round a marshy area before regaining the original track at Ketley Gate. (A little to the right, White Raise burial cairn is worthy of attention.) Cross the wide track, continuing virtually straight ahead on an ascending path. Turn left at a grassy crossing of paths, making directly for the top left corner of a walled wood above. From here head left along the edge of the high ground and then, almost immediately, bear right along a wide path through the bracken. Keep left at a fork to find the little cairn at the top of Heughscar Hill. The flat summit occupies a commanding position, offering rewarding views.

8. Walk north along the high ground, keeping left when a clearer path goes right, to pass the broken little limestone crag of Heugh Scar, below to the left. At the end of the scar take a path curling down steeply to the left. Cross a track and continue down, bearing left where a faint path comes in from the right. The line of the High Street Roman road is barely discernible here. Head for the left end of a line of trees, with a huge sycamore above the corner of a stone wall. Descend steeply beside the wall. The path then swings away from the wall to rejoin the outward route just above Point 5. Turn right and return to Pooley Bridge by the same road.

Where to eat and drink

There are numerous cafés and inns in the village of Pooley Bridge. The Sun Inn is an unspoiled 18th-century coaching inn, with extensive oak beams, panelling and open fires. It offers excellent bar meals and a good selection of real ales.

What to see

The High Street Roman road is followed for a short section of this walk. In its full length, the road traverses the high eastern Lakeland fells, exceeding an altitude of 2,500ft (762m) in several places. It stretches from the Troutbeck Valley near Ambleside to Brougham by the River Eamont, where it intercepts the main southeast–northwest Roman arterial road. It is a remarkable testament to the ambition of Roman engineering.

While you're there

Just beyond Pooley Bridge, the shores of Ullswater, the region's second largest lake – some 7.5 miles (12km) long – are a fine place to contemplate the beauty of the Lake District. Five boats, including two beautifully preserved 19th-century vessels, *Lady of the Lake* and *Raven*, run regular trips from the jetty, stopping at the landing stages at Howtown, Glenridding and Aira Force.

EXPLORING UPPER KENTMERE

DISTANCE/TIME	6.75 miles (10.9km) / 2hrs 15min
ASCENT/GRADIENT	689ft (210m) / ▲
PATHS	Generally good tracks and paths, some open fields, several stiles
LANDSCAPE	Glacial valley, flood meadows, quarry workings and reservoir
SUGGESTED MAP	OS Explorer OL7 The English Lakes (SE)
START/FINISH	Grid reference: NY456040
DOG FRIENDLINESS	Farmyards and grazing land, so dogs mostly on lead
PARKING	Very limited in Kentmere, but small field by Low Bridge is occasionally available
PUBLIC TOILETS	None on route

From its source high on the slopes of Mardale Ill Bell, at the heart of Cumbria's eastern fells, the River Kent begins a journey through Kentmere, one of the country's loveliest valleys. Deep and narrow, the river follows a gently sinuous course south for some 9 miles (14.5km) before breaking free to meander between the rolling hills beyond Staveley. In its higher reaches the Kent is isolated from frenetic modern life, and there is a wonderful sense of remoteness as you wander below towering crags. From earliest times, the dale has supported small communities who made a living by farming the confined valley bottoms and lower slopes. Perhaps the pickings were never very great, but it must still have been a tempting target for raiders (known as reivers) from the north, who could ride over the pass from Mardale, grab what they might find, and be away again before an alarm could be raised.

The hall at Kentmere was built by the Gilpins around the 14th century, as a square, battlemented tower rising over a vaulted basement. A narrow spiral staircase was the only access to the upper floors, a further obstacle to any aggressor who managed to burst through the heavily barred door. With their cattle and sheep safely inside, the family could easily defend themselves. The trouble across this area continued after the defeat of the Scots at Flodden in 1513, and it was not until James VI of Scotland succeeded to the English throne almost 100 years later that the raiding way of life ended. However, some security must have been felt before then, since a farmhouse was added in the 16th century and the tower became an outhouse or barn. Some of Kentmere Hall's occupants earned a reputation extending far beyond the lonely valley. Hugh Herd, who acquired the title of the 'Cork Lad of Kentmere', was a giant of a man. Born to a nun at Furness Abbey, he became a champion wrestler and served King Edward VI, repelling invaders back across the border with Scotland. More dubious was Richard Gilpin, said to have killed the last wild boar in England.

8

STAVELEY'S MILL YARD AND CRAGGY WOOD

DISTANCE/TIME	4 miles (6.4km) / 2hrs
ASCENT/GRADIENT	558ft (170m) / ▲ ▲
PATHS	Woodland and grassy paths and tracks, road, 6 stiles
LANDSCAPE	Village, woods and fields
SUGGESTED MAP	OS Explorer OL7 The English Lakes (SE)
START/FINISH	Grid reference: SD470983
DOG FRIENDLINESS	Fields grazed by sheep, otherwise reasonably suitable for dogs
PARKING	On-street parking around Staveley Main Street, or in Mill Yard
PUBLIC TOILETS	Beside bus stop in Abbey Square, Staveley

It's no coincidence that this walk starts and finishes by the modern-day buildings of Staveley Mill Yard. The history of the village and its surrounding area is closely linked to the fortunes of the mills that developed on the banks of the River Kent – at its peak, there were 30 mills drawing power from the river. There may have been a fulling mill here, processing local wool, as early as the 14th century, but it was wood that really drove the industry on. In the 1820s local entrepreneur Thomas Taylor realised that the opening of the Lancaster Canal to nearby Kendal presented an opportunity. The booming Lancashire cotton mills needed vast quantities of bobbins – reels and spindles. Staveley had woodlands and water power to drive machines, and soon Taylor had 24 lathes and four saws, taking power from a waterwheel. Taylor himself didn't live long enough to enjoy the prosperity, succumbing to the cholera epidemic of 1832, but the mill went from strength to strength. In 1853 Chadwick's of Bolton bought the mill and adjacent land, widened the River Kent and built a new weir (the one you can see today). Edwin Brockbank, himself the son of a bobbin turner became owner of the mill in 1946 and the site is still owned by the third generation of Brockbanks, although all production here ceased in the 1990s.

The mill yard reborn
So far, the narrative is typical of British industrial growth and decline, but the story of the mill site doesn't end there. The coppice sheds, where wood was stacked and dried, now house a number of light industrial units. Other parts of the mill have been redeveloped, and, as well as the Hawkshead Brewery, outdoor clothing suppliers, artisan food and wine outlets, cafés and offices have moved in. Up to 15 per cent of the yard's power still comes from turbines driven by the waters of the River Kent. The coppiced woods across the river are now managed by wildlife charities and the National Park Authority, and Staveley has been reinvented as a thoroughly modern, sustainable community.

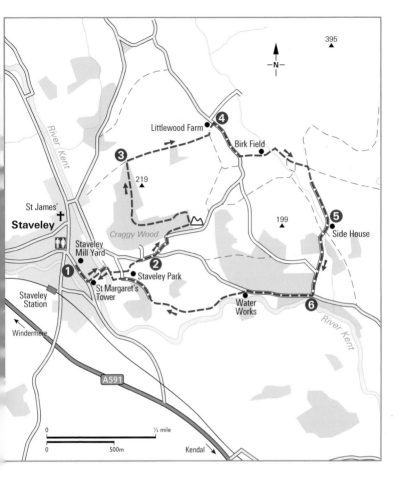

1. Walk down Main Street, heading southeast to reach the old tower of
St Margaret's Church. A footpath runs down the side of the churchyard and
along the back of the Mill Yard. At the river, cross the bridge and follow the
path beyond to the right. Turn left, at the corner of the wall, and go through a
kissing gate between farm buildings. Continue straight ahead through a gate to
the right of a barn, and keep a wall on your left as you pass through trees and
another gate to a minor road. Turn right to a junction.

2. Turn left up the hill and, at a right-hand bend, dodge left into Craggy Wood.
The single path is obvious and first takes you parallel with the road before
swinging steeply up to the left towards the crest of the woods. At the highest
point a magnificent view is revealed of the fells around Kentmere. Stay with
the path through the woods as it undulates, trending downhill slightly, to
emerge suddenly at a stile into a field.

3. Turn right here, through a gap. Keep a wall on your left and aim for a stile
that appears on the skyline. Beyond this, maintain your direction across the
field to find a ladder stile. Continue down the next field with a wall on your left,
to a stile, beyond which the wall is now on your right. Keep to this as you

descend to Littlewood Farm. Approaching the farm, follow the fence left then go through a gate into the farmyard.

4. Now join a lane and turn right. Go through a gate and continue on this minor road until a footpath sign ('Potter Tarn') points left down a farm access track. Walk down the track, then through a gate, following the arrow across the yard and through another gate to pass in front of the farmhouse. Now a short stretch of enclosed track crosses a tiny beck. Turn right alongside it, then emerge through a gate into a field. The path follows the beck before heading away alongside a plantation then up a rough field to a gate. Turn right beyond this to join a descending track, ignoring a path left to Potter Tarn, to Side House.

5. Join the access track to cross the beck then follow the track through a couple of gates. Keep straight ahead at a junction and descend to meet a tarmac lane at a bend. Keep ahead, down the road, to a T-junction in the valley bottom.

6. Turn right along this for 0.25 miles (400m). By the entrance to a sewage treatment works, take a footpath across a paddock then continue to a gate by the river. Follow the obvious meadow path to a ladder stile. Bear right from this, then left after some hawthorn trees to a gate under trees in the far corner. An enclosed lane now leads you in front of Staveley Park. Go through a gate and straight ahead to rejoin the outward route along the riverside and back into the town.

Where to eat and drink

Staveley Mill Yard is a wondrous place. The Beer Hall is Hawkshead Brewery's showcase, where you can sample all their brews, and put your nose to the glass to see them in production. Next door is Wilf's Café, a legendary purveyor of locally sourced traditional café fare. Just round the corner is More?, an artisan baker and coffee shop. At all three you can sit outside and watch cyclists testing their potential new bikes.

What to see

St Margaret's church tower is prominent at the start of this walk. Dating from the 14th century, by the middle of the 19th the church was in a very poor state of repair. A new vicar, arriving in 1858, was horrified and set about raising money to build a new church. St James's opened in 1865 at the other end of the village in a much drier location, and included stained glass by Edward Burne-Jones in its east window. Of the old church, only St Margaret's tower and the churchyard were retained, the former restored to mark Queen Victoria's Golden Jubilee in 1887.

While you're there

Windermere – the town, not the lake – is a short way west. Taking a bus or train saves parking worries at the end. The ever-popular short walk up Orrest Head starts a stone's throw from the station. The view from here was legendary guidebook writer Alfred Wainwright's first sight of the Lakeland Fells.

ALONG THE LIMESTONE OF CUNSWICK SCAR

DISTANCE/TIME	3 miles (4.8km) / 1hr 30min
ASCENT/GRADIENT	250ft (76m) / ▲ ▲
PATHS	Paths and tracks, can be muddy – take care as edge of scar is unguarded in places
LANDSCAPE	Fields and open fell along high limestone shoulder
SUGGESTED MAP	OS Explorer OL7 The English Lakes (SE)
START/FINISH	Grid reference: SD489923
DOG FRIENDLINESS	Fellside grazed by sheep; dogs must be under control
PARKING	Beneath radio mast near top of hill (Cunswick car park not the Scout Scar car park)
PUBLIC TOILETS	None on route

At the southwestern boundary of the Lake District National Park, Cunswick Scar is a high shoulder of white Carboniferous limestone running from north to south. Its southern end links with Scout Scar, although a geological fault, taken by the high Underbarrow Road, has displaced the whole of Scout Scar westwards from the northern leg of Cunswick Scar and Cunswick Fell. From the east, gently sloping fellside rises to a height of 680ft (207m), before falling suddenly in a vertical face to present a long and spectacular cliff running above the woods and pastures of Underbarrow. The effect is dramatic, and the tops of both Cunswick Scar and Scout Scar present wonderful views over Kentdale and the Lyth Valley, extending outwards to the Lakeland fells, Morecambe Bay and the distant hills of the Yorkshire Dales.

Carboniferous limestone

The naked white bones of both these scars are composed of pure Carboniferous limestone. This attractive alkaline rock, which has provided the building material for most of the nearby town of Kendal, is home to a rich flora and fauna and noted for its splendid fossils. It was formed some 270–350 million years ago when a warm, shallow sea covered the central dome of Lakeland. Living in its waters were corals, brachiopods (shellfish), molluscs, gastropods (snails) and colonies of crinoids – sometimes referred to as sea lilies. The shell-like remains of these animals sank to the bottom of the seabed and, over the aeons, accumulated into thick layers or beds. These beds compacted together and solidified to form the brilliant white limestone we see exposed today. By the end of the Carboniferous period the Lake District was buried under several thousand feet of limestone. A period of uplifting and folding, followed by arid desert conditions, stripped down through the limestone layers until, finally, the glaciation of the Ice Age (the last glacial retreat ending around 15,000 years ago) gouged, shattered and polished

Cunswick Scar into the outline shape we see now. The more recent effects of freeze and thaw shattering has added the banks of scree seen to the west, beneath the scar. The dissolving action of carbonic acid, produced by endless rainwater, has resulted in the columns (clints) and deep vertical fissures (grykes) of the limestone pavements along the top of the scar. The west face of the scar, overlooking the mixed woods, emerald fields and the scattered white farmsteads of the Lyth and Underbarrow valleys, contrasts markedly with the starkness of the plateau above. On these cliffs, alongside the tenacious yew and pine that have forced their way into secure rocky crannies, brightly coloured flowers abound in summertime. In June the prevailing colour of these flowers is yellow. Spreads of common rock rose, hoary rock rose, horseshoe vetch and hawkweed drape the rock ledges and look particularly striking against the grey-white of the limestone and the dark green foliage of the yew.

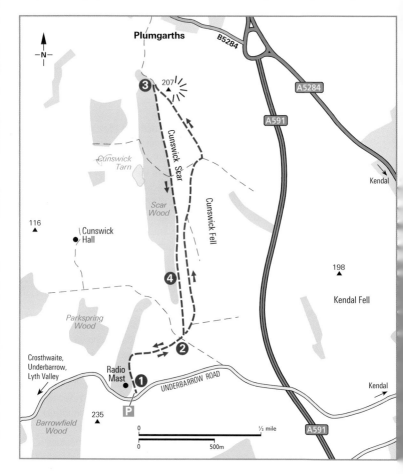

1. Walk away from the road, cross the sloping limestone bed that forms the car park and take the track with the barrier across it that leads to the radio mast. Follow the narrow path through the trees. Leave the woods by a kissing gate at the junction of the stone walls by a footpath sign for Cunswick Fell.

Enter the field and continue beside the stone wall on the left. On reaching the corner of the field go right and follow the path parallel to the wall. Continue over the humpback of the field and drop to pass a gate, beyond which the wall turns a sharp corner.

2. Continue ahead on a grassy path for 30yds (27m), then follow it round to the left, aiming for a lone fingerpost. Ignore the right turn here, staying with the track over the brow and down to a gate in a fence. Go through the gate and follow the wall on the right as it descends to a dip. Keep straight ahead as the wall bends right beyond the dip. On drawing level with a stile in the wall, turn left on a more prominent track. Follow this to the top of the hill, where you'll find the summit cairn of Cunswick Scar, a commanding viewpoint.

3. Walk northwest beyond the cairn and drop to the lower terrace edged by the scar. Take care here – the cliff face of the scar is unfenced at this point and reaches a vertical height of around 40ft (12m). Turn left, heading south along the edge of the scar. A fence soon runs along the edge of the crag. Keep along the rim of the scar through an avenue of juniper and hazel to the end of a wall. Keep to the path beside the wall to a small gate.

4. The path continues by the wall, swinging away from it briefly, before returning to the wall corner passed earlier. Turn right, retracing your steps by following the line of the wall all the way round to the kissing gate at the edge of the wood. Keep left at an early fork through the trees to return to the car park.

Where to eat and drink

Kendal is nearby and offers a huge choice. Underbarrow and the Lyth Valley lie to the east, with a number of quaint little inns that offer bar meals. Nearest to the scar are the Punch Bowl Inn at Crosthwaite and the Black Labrador at Underbarrow.

What to see

There are many fossils in the limestone of Cunswick Scar and Cunswick Fell. Particularly attractive are the corals, and there are at least three varieties to be found. The largest of these is the colonial coral, which may form clumps of up to 1ft (30cm) in diameter. Molluscs are well represented and gastropods (snails) are abundant. Sometimes it is the hard calcium shell of the snail that has been preserved, while on other occasions it is the spiralling softer inner body of the snail.

While you're there

To the west of the scar the quiet Underbarrow and the Lyth Valley are worthy of exploration. The Lyth Valley particularly is noted for its damson trees. In springtime its white blossom resembles winter snows, and in autumn its annual harvest is used for jam or wine making.

HIGH ARNSIDE KNOTT

DISTANCE/TIME	5.5 miles (8.8km) / 3hrs
ASCENT/GRADIENT	560ft (171m) / ▲
PATHS	Foreshore (tide permitting), paths, some surfaced road, 1 stile
LANDSCAPE	Estuary and foreshore, mixed woods, limestone knoll
SUGGESTED MAP	OS Explorer OL7 The English Lakes (SE)
START/FINISH	Grid reference: SD456787
DOG FRIENDLINESS	Generally a good walk for energetic dogs
PARKING	Along Promenade or in Arnside Beach car park near the viaduct
PUBLIC TOILETS	On Lower Promenade
NOTES	Parts of foreshore impassable at high tide, beware of rapidly incoming tides and quicksand; some unguarded little crags

Rising from the Kent estuary to form a defiant outpost of resilient limestone, the heights of Arnside Knott are part of the Arnside-Silverdale Area of Outstanding Natural Beauty. Bedecked with magnificent oak and mixed woods, rocky scree, hummocky grass, scattered bushes and the airy delights of steep open hillside, the hills also have the salty tang of the Kent Estuary, which floods out into Morecambe Bay. Above the trees, to the north, the panoramic view of the high fells of Lakeland is spectacular. There are many spots where you can enjoy this view, but none better than the toposcope (view indicator) below and west of the summit.

On the sands

The little town of Arnside, with its station, viaduct crossing the estuary, and elegant white limestone buildings, exudes a quiet feeling of Victorian affluence. Local children used to be thrilled by the tales of the Arnside Bore, a wave that runs in at the front of a rising tide; it still presents a dramatic sight but also great danger out on the sands, as the tide floods in at a gallop. A warning siren is sounded at the start of an incoming tide – heed its call.

On selected days every summer, Arnside is also the starting point for the famous Cross-Bay Walks. Usually hundreds take part, following the guide on a carefully planned course across the sands of Morecambe Bay, wading through channels to come ashore at Kents Bank for the 10-minute return journey by train. The ever-shifting sands mean that the route is never exactly the same twice. It's all done for pleasure now, but before the days of roads and railways this was a regular route of travel. The dangers were such that the office of Queen's Guide to the Sands was created in 1548. Cedric Robinson died in Nov 2021, having retired in 2019 after 56 years. The current holder of the King's Guide to the Sands is Michael Wilson.

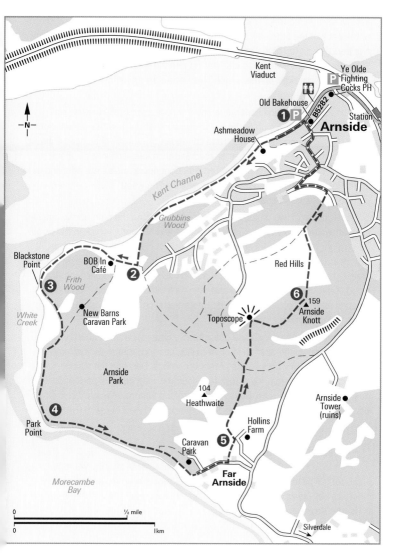

1. Walk along the promenade. At the end of the surfaced road, by the entrance to Ashmeadow House, a walkway to the right continues above the sands. Continue along the path until it joins the foreshore. Continuing beneath Grubbins Wood, the path crosses mud, pebbles and a polished limestone outcrop before it rounds a little headland to join a track. Depending on the tide, it may seem attractive to walk along the sands on the foreshore. This isn't recommended as quicksands are prevalent here and are undetectable until you sink.

2. Turn right to New Barns Caravan Park; before the buildings, bear right past a barrier, initially following a clear track and then along the foreshore. Round Frith Wood, following the path beneath the trees, high on the pebble beach. Keep on to rocky Blackstone Point. You may have to wait to round it if the tide is high.

3. Having rounded Blackstone Point, enter the little bay of White Creek. Keep to the back of the little bay, past a shingle bank and a limestone outcrop with two benches on top of it. About 150yds (137m) beyond this outcrop, a break in the low cliffs allows you to clamber up into the trees and join a reasonably clear path. Turn right on this – along the coastal fringe of the woods of Arnside Park.

4. Round Park Point and continue along the edge. Eventually a stone wall slants up the slope. Go up to the left to join another track in the woods, signed 'Far Arnside, Silverdale'. Go right and continue through the gate, soon entering a caravan site. Take the left, higher road and then keep straight on, along Pebble Row and Cliff Drive, to exit the site. Continue to a squeeze stile and gate on the left, signed 'Public Footpath Arnside via The Knott'. Follow the fenced path to Hollins Farm and exit by a stile.

5. Go left through two gates, then bear right, following the path up the hillside of Heathwaite. A gate leads through the wall and out onto a track in the woods. Go straight across and ascend the stony track, curving up a steep section. At a fork bear left, soon reaching a little gate. Once through this, bear right to climb steeply to the toposcope. Follow the path through a gate and back into the wood. Keep to the clearest path and then turn left at a junction. Continue up to a bench near the summit of Arnside Knott. Paths on the right lead to the trig point, hidden by trees.

6. Bear left from the bench and descend to a gate in a wall. Follow a wide green path down the open field of Red Hills, bearing right to the bottom corner of the field where a gate enters the woods. Descend the track through the woods to a road. Turn left; soon the road doubles back and descends to a larger road. Go right along this to Silverdale Road. Turn left down to the seafront.

Where to eat and drink
Ye Olde Fighting Cocks, a traditional inn whose name tells its own tale about the history of the region, is situated centrally on the seafront and offers bar meals and real ales. Also on the front, near the end of the walk, is the Old Bakehouse.

What to see
The oak woods, open tussocky grassland and scrub of this high limestone knoll are noted for their butterflies; some 27 species are regularly seen. Of particular interest are Scotch argus, on the wing between July and early August, and the high brown fritillary, in late June or early July.

While you're there
Arnside Tower, which you might glimpse over to the east as you climb the slopes of Heathwaite, is an ancient pele tower, built to shelter the locals against the marauding Scots. The danger was real: in 1322, during the Great Raid, Robert the Bruce ravaged Cartmel and burned down Lancaster. Reacting to these events, the Harrington family built this tower in 1375. It burned down in 1602. Though rebuilt, it was abandoned to its fate sometime after 1684; it's now crumbling and unsafe to enter.

OVER HAMPSFELL ABOVE GRANGE-OVER-SANDS

DISTANCE/TIME	4 miles (6.4km) / 1hr 45min
ASCENT/GRADIENT	790ft (241m) / ▲ ▲ ▲
PATHS	Paths and tracks, exposed limestone (slippery when wet), 4 stiles
LANDSCAPE	Town, woods and open fell, extensive seascapes
SUGGESTED MAP	OS Explorer OL7 The English Lakes (SE)
START/FINISH	Grid reference: SD410780
DOG FRIENDLINESS	Busy lanes and open fell grazed by sheep
PARKING	Off Main Street by Ornamental Gardens or at railway station
PUBLIC TOILETS	At Ornamental Gardens and near Clock Tower

TAKE NOTICE
All persons visiting this 'hospice' by permission of the owner, are requested to respect private property, and not by acts of wanton mischief and destruction show that they possess more muscle than brain. I have no hope that this request will be attended to, for as Solomon says 'Though thou shouldest bray a fool in a mortar among wheat with a pestle, yet will not his foolishness depart from him'.

So reads one of the panels inside the peculiar Hospice of Hampsfell at the high point of this walk. Its tone matches that of Grange-over-Sands, with its neat and tidy white limestone buildings, colourful gardens, sunny aspect and seaside disposition. It has long been a popular seaside resort, particularly since the arrival of the Furness Railway in 1857. Day-trippers would also arrive by steamer via Morecambe Bay. They disembarked at the Claire House Pier, which was dramatically blown away by a storm in 1928. Today the sea is somewhat distanced from the sea wall and the town has fallen from grace with many holiday-makers. Nonetheless, it retains a refined air of quiet dignity, and its Ornamental Gardens, complete with ponds, provide a gentle prelude to the walk. The route then rises to the open, airy spaces of Hampsfell via the charming mixed woods of Eggerslack, which add yet another dimension to this pleasant area.

The Hospice of Hampsfell
Built of dressed limestone blocks, the neat square tower that adorns the top of Hampsfell is known as the Hospice of Hampsfell. It was apparently built by a minister from nearby Cartmel Priory over a century ago for 'the shelter and entertainment of travellers over the fell'. Enclosed by a fence of chains supported by small stone pillars to keep cattle out, and with an entrance door and three windows, it provides a convenient shelter should the weather take a turn for the worse. On its north face, stone steps guarded by an iron handrail

provide access to the top of the tower, and a splendid view. On the top, a novel direction indicator – consisting of a wooden sighting arrow mounted on a rotating circular table – lets you know which distant point of interest you are looking at. Simply align the arrow to the chosen subject, read the angle created by the arrow and locate it on the list on the east rail.

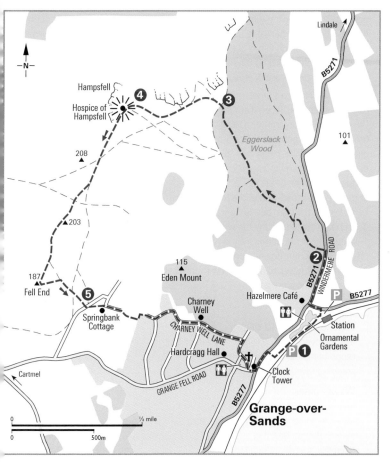

1. From the exit end of the car park enter the Ornamental Gardens. Take the right-hand path for better views (or go left if you wish to use the toilets). Exit to a roundabout and go up Windermere Road. After a slight left bend, find steps up to a squeeze stile on the left, signed 'Routon Well/Hampsfield'.

2. Take the path rising through Eggerslack Wood. Cross directly over a surfaced track and continue to pass a house on the left. Steps lead on to a second track. Cross this diagonally to follow a track, signed 'Hampsfell'. The track zigzags left then right. Keep straight on at a path junction to a stile in a wall.

3. Cross the stile to leave the wood and follow the path directly up the hillside, soon bearing slightly left. Pass sections of limestone pavement and little

craggy outcrops, then cross a stile over a stone wall. Turn right along the wall, and at the corner bear slightly right, following a grassy track, to pass ancient stone cairns and up to the obvious square tower of the Hospice of Hampsfell.

4. Turn left at the tower and follow the path over the edge of a little limestone escarpment (take care here). Continue over another escarpment and gently down to a stile. Keep straight ahead, through a dip and up the green hill beyond. Cross over the top and descend to a gate and stile in a wall. Although the path bears left here it is usual to continue directly to the prominent cairn on Fell End, with fine views over Morecambe Bay. Turn sharp left to rejoin the main path, which skirts to the left of a little tree-filled valley and descends to a gate on to a road by stock pens.

5. Cross the road to a small gate and descend diagonally left across the field to a gate onto a surfaced track (by the front door of Springbank Cottage). Descend the track to enter a farmyard and bear right to a stone stile. Go over the hill, following the path alongside the wall and cross a stile into a narrow ginnel (alley). With a high wall to the right, follow this down and round the corner and descend to a junction of roads. Go left on a private road/public footpath, and then bear right on a stony track. At the next junction turn right to descend the road, and at the following junction go left down Charney Well Lane. Where the road bends right, go straight ahead on a smaller road, descending steeply below the woods of Eden Mount. When you reach a T-junction near the bottom of the hill, turn right. At the junction with a larger road, go left (toilets opposite) and pass the church before descending past the clock tower to a junction with the main road (B5277). Go left and then right to the car park.

Where to eat and drink

Grange-over-Sands has many excellent cafés and inns catering for a wide range of tastes. The Hazelmere Café, near the start/finish, is a long-standing favourite that hasn't rested on its laurels.

What to see

Rising skyward above the main street and below the church, the clock tower is noted as one of the finest buildings in Grange. It was financed by Mrs Sophia Deardon and built in 1912 from local limestone (probably from the quarry at Eden Mount), and the lovely chocolate-brown St Bees sandstone.

While you're there

If you look up Grange Fell Road out of Grange you will see an impressive white limestone building. Hardcragg Hall is the oldest house in Grange and is dated 1563. John Wilkinson, ironmaster, once lived here. His first iron boat was launched some 2 miles (3.2km) away at Castlehead, on the River Winster.

BRANT FELL ABOVE BOWNESS-ON-WINDERMERE

DISTANCE/TIME	3.5 miles (5.7km) / 1hr 15min
ASCENT/GRADIENT	525ft (160m) / ▲ ▲
PATHS	Pavement, road, stony tracks, grassy paths, several stiles
LANDSCAPE	Town, mixed woodland, open fell, lake and fell views
SUGGESTED MAP	OS Explorer OL7 The English Lakes (SE)
START/FINISH	Grid reference: SD398966
DOG FRIENDLINESS	Popular route for dogs; busy roads and sheep grazing, so must be under control
PARKING	Car park on Glebe Road above Windermere lake
PUBLIC TOILETS	Near information centre at end of Glebe Road

Walking from the honeypot of Bowness-on-Windermere on a busy summer weekend, it is hard to imagine that just above the lakeside bustle there is a world of quiet solitude and space. With relatively little effort, however, you can crest the heights of Brant Fell and enjoy a wonderful, lonely view out over Windermere to the Coniston fells, the Langdale Pikes and the mighty Fairfield.

Bowness-on-Windermere
Fed by the high rainfall of the Lake District fells, via the rivers Brathay, Rothay and Troutbeck, Windermere is England's largest natural lake, stretching some 10.5 miles (16.9km) from Waterhead to Lakeside. It is up to 0.9 miles (1.45km) wide in places, and reaches a depth of 220ft (67m), so its ice-scoured bed is well below sea level. Overlooked by this walk, the privately owned Belle Isle is said to have been used since Roman times. Today this island is supplied by a little boat, which serves the 38-acre (15ha) estate. Belle Isle's interesting circular house, restored after extensive fire damage in 1996, was originally erected by Mr English in 1774. Apparently William Wordsworth credited Mr English with the honour of being the first man to settle in the Lake District for the sake of the scenery. There have been many more since. The main gateway and access point to the lake, Bowness-on-Windermere, is the most popular holiday destination in the Lake District. More than 10,000 boats are registered on the lake. Once the Oxenholme–Kendal–Windermere railway opened in 1847 the town developed rapidly. Windermere town grew around the station from what was once a small village called Birthwaite. The railway company named the station Windermere to attract trade, although it is some distance from the lake. In the late 19th century wealthy businessmen, principally from industrial towns in Lancashire, built luxurious residences overlooking the lake. Many of these are now hotels, while Brockhole is now the National Park Visitor Centre

and Blackwell is owned by the Lakeland Arts Trust and open for visitors. The Belsfield Hotel, overlooking Bowness Bay, was bought in 1860 by Henry Schneider, the chairman of the prosperous Barrow Steelworks and Shipworks. Reputedly he left home each morning and boarded his steam yacht *Esperance*, taking breakfast whilst travelling down the lake to Lakeside. He then journeyed by steam train – he owned the railway and had his own private carriage – to the works in Barrow.

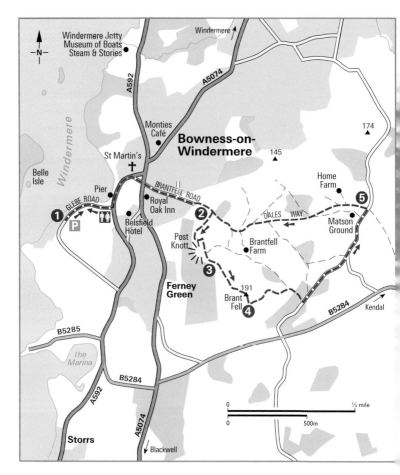

1. Take Glebe Road into Bowness town. Swing left to follow the main Windermere road, crossing opposite the steamer pier. Opposite the impressive St Martin's Church, turn right to ascend the little street of St Martin's Hill. Cross the Kendal road to climb Brantfell Road directly above. At the head of the road a little iron gate leads on to the Dales Way, a grassy and stony path that climbs directly up the hillside. Continue to a kissing gate by the wood, leading onto a lane.

2. Pass through the kissing gate and turn right, signposted 'Post Knott', to follow the stony lane. Continue on the lane rising through the woods until it crests a height near the flat, circular top of Post Knott. Bear left and make the

short ascent to the summit. The view from here was once exceptional but is now obscured by trees. Retrace a few steps towards the track, bearing left to find a kissing gate leading out of the wood onto the open hillside.

3. Beyond the kissing gate take the wide path to a bench on a rocky shoulder. Bear left, and first descend, then ascend to a gate in the corner below a gap in the trees. Cross the stile, then bear right to ascend directly up the open grassy flanks of Brant Fell to its rocky summit.

4. Go left from the summit, then look for a line of cairns. Follow these down to a kissing gate. Descend through a plantation to a second gate and a track. Turn right and follow the track to a stile. Turn left down to a road, then left along it. Keep left at the next junction. Immediately beyond Matson Ground house and farm is a kissing gate on the left, waymarked for the Dales Way.

5. Go through the kissing gate and continue down the path to cross a track via two kissing gates. Keep along the path beneath trees and beside a pond, until the path swings left to emerge through a kissing gate onto a surfaced drive. Go right along the drive for 30yds (27m) until the path veers off left through the trees to follow the fence. An iron gate leads into a field. Follow the grassy path, first descending and then rising to an iron kissing gate in the corner of the field. Continue to another gate leading into a walled track. Cross the surfaced drive of Brantfell Farm and keep straight on to a gate leading into a field. Follow the path alongside the wall, descending the hill to intercept a track, via a kissing gate, coming again to Point 2. Retrace your steps back to Glebe Road.

Where to eat and drink

Bowness-on-Windermere is inundated with cafés, inns, shops and restaurants. Conveniently located near the start and finish of the route, at the foot of Brantfell Road, is the Royal Oak Inn. In the town centre, Monties café bar is an established favourite.

What to see

St Martin's Church, an impressive building surrounded by ancient yew trees, is the parish church of Bowness, built in 1483 and restored and enlarged in 1870. It is well worth taking a look inside. Behind the church is the oldest area of Bowness, known as Lowside, an intriguing web of narrow streets among buildings of dark slate.

While you're there

Quite apart from the natural beauty of the area, there is plenty to see and do around Bowness. Windermere Jetty Museum of Boats, Steam and Stories, just north of the town, is well worth a visit, and has a fabulous café overlooking the lake. South of Bowness, just off the B5360, stands Blackwell, a truly beautiful house from the early 20th century. Blackwell embodies the principles of the Arts and Crafts Movement, a reaction against the advance of industrialisation and mechanisation. There's an excellent café and gift shop too.

PATTERDALE
TO SILVER POINT

DISTANCE/TIME	4 miles (6.4km) / 1hr 30min
ASCENT/GRADIENT	620ft (190m) / ▲▲
PATHS	Stony tracks and paths
LANDSCAPE	Lake and fell views, mixed woodland
SUGGESTED MAP	OS Explorer OL5 The English Lakes (NE)
START/FINISH	Grid reference: NY396159
DOG FRIENDLINESS	Passes through working farm and open hillside grazed by sheep, so dogs must be under control at all times
PARKING	Pay-and-display car park opposite Patterdale Hotel
PUBLIC TOILETS	Opposite White Lion Inn in Patterdale village centre

The elongated hamlet of Patterdale has a rugged, mountain quality. Sited below the mighty Helvellyn massif, its collection of stone buildings have a starkness about them. This makes a perfect contrast to the splendour of Ullswater, whose southern shore lies hardly a stone's throw away. This walk strolls through mixed woodland and open aspect above the shores of the lake to visit the famed viewpoint of Silver Point. The adventurous may wish to make the detour to the top of Silver Crag, as did horsedrawn coach parties of old, for a better view of the lake. Alfred Wainwright (1907–91), known for his seven *Pictorial Guides to the Lakeland Fells*, regarded this to be a part of one of the most beautiful walks in the Lakes.

Ullswater
Undoubtedly one of the loveliest of the lakes, the three legs of Ullswater add up to a total length of 7.5 miles (12.1km), with an average width of 0.5 miles (800m) and a maximum depth of 205ft (62.5m). It is Lakeland's second largest lake after Windermere. Its waters are exceptionally clear and in the deepest part of the lake, off Howtown, lives a curious fish called the schelly – a creature akin to a freshwater herring. Apart from rescue and Park Ranger launches, you won't see many power boats here, but Ullswater Steamers have up to five boats operating between Glenridding and Pooley Bridge all year round. Preservation of the lake in its present form is due to a concerted campaign, led in parliament by Lord Birkett, against the proposed Manchester Corporation Water Act in 1965. Although the act was passed, and water is extracted from the lake, the workings are hidden underground and designed in such a way as to make it impossible to lower the water level beyond the agreed limit. It was the golden yellow daffodils of Glencoyne, on the northern shore opposite Silver Point, that inspired William Wordsworth's most widely known poem, 'I wandered lonely as a cloud' (published in 1807). His sister

Dorothy described them vividly in her diary: 'I never saw daffodils so beautiful. They grew among the mossy stones about and around them, some rested their heads upon these stones as on a pillar for weariness and the rest tossed and reeled and danced and seemed as if they verily laughed with the wind that blew them over the lake.'

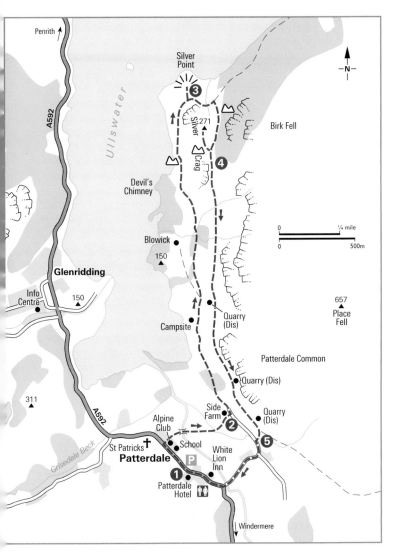

1. From the car park walk to the road and turn right. Pass the school and take the track leading off right, beside the Alpine Club hut. Follow the track over a bridge and continue through the buildings of Side Farm to join another track.

2. Turn left along the track, with a stone wall to the left. Pass through mixed woodland, predominantly oak and ash, before open fellside appears above. Continue above the campsite, and pass a large cairn-cum-seat below a stand

of larches before descending to cross a little stream. The path ascends again to crest a craggy knoll above the woods of Devil's Chimney. Make a steep descent before the path levels to traverse beneath the craggy heights of Silver Crag. A slight ascent gains the shoulder of Silver Point and an outstanding view of Ullswater. A short there-and-back to the tip is worthwhile.

3. Follow the path beneath the end of Silver Crag, and descend to a marker post where a steep pitched path breaks off to the right. Ascend this, climbing through the juniper bushes. Gain the narrow gap that separates Silver Crag, on the right, from the main hillside of Birk Fell on the left. This little valley is quite boggy and holds a small tarnlet. At its end is a low grassy saddle.

4. The adventurous can enjoy a short detour here to the top of Silver Crag for a wonderful view, but care must be exercised for steep ground lies in every direction. For the detour, take a faint trail to the right as you approach the saddle. When it splits, bear right again to fight your way through the juniper on a steep, rocky trail, to the summit. Descend back to the small valley and the main path by the same route. The main walk continues over the saddle and along an easy path, traversing the open fellside. Pass open quarry workings, where there is a large unfenced hole next to the path (take care). Descend slightly then bear left at a level spot overlooking Side Farm. Climb slightly and cross the spoil of a larger, tree-filled quarry. Descend to a little footbridge leading to a gate.

5. Go through the gate and turn left along the lane. Keep right at a junction, cross the bridge and join the road. Bear right through Patterdale to return to the car park.

Where to eat and drink
En route, Side Farm sometimes offers teas and ice creams. In the centre of Patterdale the White Lion Inn serves bar meals throughout the year. The village shop, opposite, has a range of hot and cold snacks and a 'snack shack' in which to eat them.

What to see
The distinctive golden yellow and white of the indigenous daffodil still abounds in the woods by the lake shore and may be seen at their best from mid-March to mid-April. This wild variety is smaller than the broader-flowered cultivated version and, many would say, even more lovely. There has been concern recently that the introduction of cultivated daffodils to this area is actually damaging the survival prospects of its smaller relative and jeopardising the view Wordsworth loved.

While you're there
Take a look around the nearby village of Glenridding. It has an information centre, inns and a variety of shops and places of interest. It is now the main gateway to the high Helvellyn massif, and a popular place for hillwalkers and climbers. Until the 1960s it was also an important mining village. The Greenside Lead Mine, located at the top of the valley, was the largest lead mine in Britain. All is now quiet, and a youth hostel occupies a former mine building.

WATERFALLS AT AIRA FORCE

DISTANCE/TIME	3 miles (4.8km) / 2hrs
ASCENT/GRADIENT	460ft (140m) / ▲
PATHS	Stony paths, steps and surfaced road
LANDSCAPE	Pinetum, tree-lined river gorge, woods and open meadow
SUGGESTED MAP	OS Explorer OL5 The English Lakes (NE)
START/FINISH	Grid reference: NY400200
DOG FRIENDLINESS	Under very good control; narrow paths with steep drops, sheep pastures and open road
PARKING	National Trust's Aira Force pay-and-display car park, off A592
PUBLIC TOILETS	At Aira Force car park

This circular walk climbs the tree-clad gorge of Aira Beck to pass two waterfalls before continuing to ascend through natural woodland and meadows to the hamlet of Dockray. The lower, larger waterfall, Aira Force, is the more famous of the two. It offers an impressive sight from the viewpoint stone bridges above and below the falls. The beck cascades some 70ft (21m) vertically down a narrow, rocky chasm into the pool beneath the lower bridge. The view directly down the chasm and waterfall from the upper bridge is breathtaking, and not for those averse to heights. Aira Force was mentioned several times by Wordsworth, notably in 'The Somnambulist':

> Doth Aira-force, that torrent hoarse,
> Speak from the woody glen!

Particularly when in spate, the upper falls of High Force, which fall some 35ft (11m), are also impressive. Broader than Aira Force, the falls are also open to a closer approach. View them from the east bank, when ascending, from the outcropping bed of waterworn rocks above. Care must be taken, particularly when it's wet, as the rocks can be very slippery and there are no safety rails.

The area surrounding the beck is a delightful mix of pine and exotic trees. Now owned by the National Trust, it once belonged to the Howard family of Greystoke Castle, who landscaped the area around the waterfalls. In 1846 they created a pinetum and pleasure garden, planting over half a million native and ornamental trees and establishing a network of tracks, footpaths and bridges. They planted more than 200 specimen conifers, including firs, pines, spruces and cedars from all over the world. One of the most notable, passed on the walk, is a Sitka spruce from North America which now stands at around 120ft (37m) high. Higher up, towards High Force, the woods have a more natural aspect, dominated by oak trees. In the moist environment of the sheltered valley, many of the trees are thickly clad with mosses and ferns.

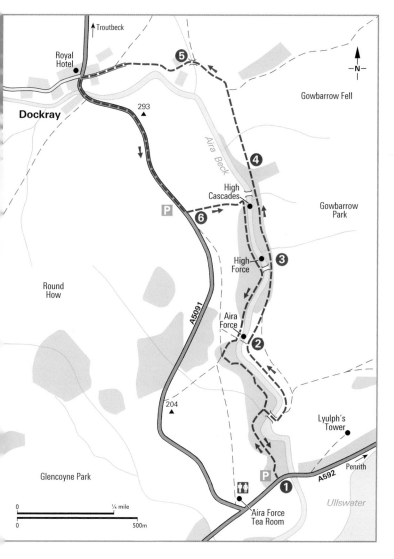

1. Head to the far end of the car park and follow the obvious path through the gap to the right of the National Trust shop. Bear right at an early fork in the path and enter the pinetum via a metal gate. This area is known as The Grove. Follow the path round to the right, over the footbridge, to cross Aira Beck. Climb the steps and fork left by the huge Sitka spruce to follow the terraced track up the east bank. At the next fork, the main route goes up the steep steps on the right, but first head left to gain the bridge at the base of Aira Force and its impressive view of the falls. At the top of the steps, keep left and you'll soon see a stone arched bridge to your left, another great place to view the falls – this time looking down on them.

2. As you continue with the beck on your left, the character of the walk changes. It's usually quieter and the path is significantly rougher. Soon after

climbing to join a path from the right, ignore the steps descending left to a wooden footbridge.

3. Continue up the main path to the delightful rocky falls of High Force. There's a viewpoint from the rocky slabs above the falls – in times of spate it is probably safest to leave a close inspection until you're on the return leg and can view High Force from the opposite (west) bank. Ignoring another wooden footbridge over Aira Beck, keep to the stony path up the east bank. Go through a stone wall to enter a small natural wood of hazel, silver birch, oak, ash, alder, rowan and sycamore. It seems light and airy compared with the denser woods found at the start of the walk.

4. Beyond the trees, the path leads easily across open ground. Pass a path to Gowbarrow Fell on your right and go through a gate. Staying with the main path, bear left at a fingerpost (towards Dockray) and cross a beck via a wooden bridge.

5. Follow the obvious track into Dockray and to a junction with the road (A5091) opposite the Royal Hotel. Turn left along the main road, and continue to a car park in an old quarry. Go through a gate on the opposite side of the road to the car park.

6. Descend the open area to another gate. Bear right above the west bank of the beck. Follow the path above the beck, later passing a wooden footbridge over a narrow ravine. Don't cross it but continue down the west bank on a clear path. As you begin climbing some steps, you'll again see the stone bridge over the top of Aira Force on your left. Just after ignoring some steps descending left, keep left at a junction, following signs for the car park. Bear left at the next fork and then turn right at a T-junction of paths in The Grove to return to the car park.

Where to eat and drink

The Aira Force Tea Room can be found next to the car park, and on a sunny day the outside benches offer a pleasant place for a cuppa or light meal. The Royal Hotel is in Dockray at the halfway point of the walk. This 16th-century coaching inn once served merchants travelling north and south across the Scottish border. Bar meals are served all year.

What to see

A short distance from the entrance to the car park, occupying a commanding position on the hillside of Gowbarrow Fell and overlooking Ullswater, stand the impressive castle-like walls of Lyulph's Tower. Although the facade of the building is a rather grand folly, the structure it incorporates is still a working farm. The building was originally a pele tower, modified by Charles Howard of Greystoke around 1780.

While you're there

There are numerous little car parks and laybys off the A592 along the northeast shore of Ullswater. They all offer pleasant places from which to paddle, swim or contemplate this most beautiful lake. In early spring there are lovely displays of wild daffodils, which inspired both Dorothy and William Wordsworth.

ACROSS THE MOSSES OF THE CALDEW

15

DISTANCE/TIME	3 miles (4.8km) / 1hr
ASCENT/GRADIENT	131ft (40m) / ▲
PATHS	Minor roads, farm tracks and grassy paths, some muddy, 5 stiles
LANDSCAPE	Open marshland valley and farmland surrounded by rough fells
SUGGESTED MAP	OS Explorer OL5 The English Lakes (NE)
START/FINISH	Grid reference: NY357319
DOG FRIENDLINESS	A few road sections and sheep in the fields means you will have your dog on lead more often than not
PARKING	Parking area on south side of the Caldew bridge in Mosedale, or in Friends Meeting House car park (donation)
PUBLIC TOILETS	None on route

This is a boundary walk, in more ways than one. Driving towards the Lake District on the A66 from Penrith, you'll barely notice the rise of the limestone uplands that form their white stone 'polo mint' around the core of the Lakeland fells. But as you enter the National Park, and drop down the bank from the junction at Troutbeck, something changes. Ahead of you the massif of Skiddaw and Blencathra rears up like an alpine vision – all pointy summits and airy ridges. This is a landscape created by glacial activity working on the underlying geology, clothed in the work of humans.

Glacial valley

The biggest change is caused by the Carrock End Fault, a geological faultline running north–south, cutting the limestone off and marking the rise of a new rock form – the Skiddaw slates. Into this gap poured millennia of glacial ice, choking the valleys with a silty debris and sculpting their sides into still more vertiginous slopes. Mosedale takes its name from the Old Norse for valley of the bog (or moss), with good reason: the River Caldew shoots out of the 'dale' part of Mosedale at a considerable pace, only to get sucked into the 'mose' part, where the raised bogs of Bowscale and Mosedale draw it in and hold it. The result is a valley where the Caldew turns sharp left to eventually reach the Eden near Carlisle, while a few paces to the right, the River Glenderamackin flows south then west to the Greta and Derwent, finally making the sea at Workington. Of all Lakeland's watersheds, this is possibly the most peculiar. You get several good glimpses of the mosses on this walk. Mosedale and Bowscale mosses form a distinct Site of Special Scientific Interest, harbouring a rich bogland ecology that is quite rare on a global scale.

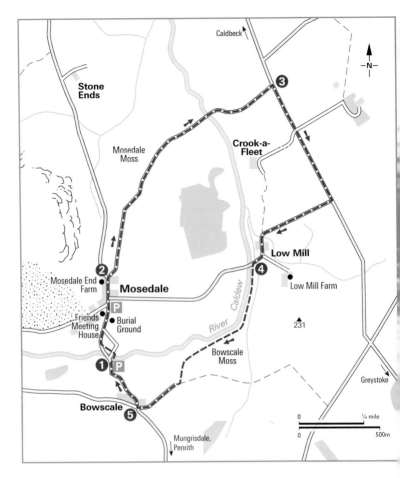

1. From the parking area, walk over the old bridge and up the grassy lane beyond to return to the road. Turn right and walk into the hamlet of Mosedale, passing the Quaker Friends Meeting House to the left with its ancient burial ground on the right (by the car park). Walk through the hamlet and opposite the last buildings (Mosedale End Farm) turn right, along a walled track sign-posted towards Hutton Roof.

2. Follow the track to a gate, beyond which it continues to the River Caldew. Cross by the footbridge and ascend the rough lane opposite, eventually to emerge at a T-junction with a minor road.

3. Turn right and follow this for 400yds (366m) – ignoring the turning for Crook-a-Fleet – to a minor lane signposted for Low Mill. Turn right down the lane, following it as it threads between farm buildings. About 100yds (91m) beyond the turning for Low Mill Farm, as you approach a bridge across the Caldew, look for a gate into the field on the left.

4. Go though this and follow the river bank levee, crossing a pair of stiles before swinging away from the river slightly to reach a stile and gate. Beyond these, stay with the left-hand edge of the field to another gate and

stile, after which a rough track leads to a further gate and stile out on to a track heading out across Bowscale Moss. Turn right up this rough lane to reach the hamlet of Bowscale.

5. At the junction with the road, turn right, following the road between the buildings and down the lane beyond, taking care as it narrows between hedges, to return to your car.

Where to eat and drink

In summer there are few places more serene or evocative than the volunteer-run tea rooms at the Friends Meeting House in Mosedale. At other times of the year, or if you're in need of something more substantial, the Mill Inn at Mungrisdale offers a full menu of bar and restaurant food, and keeps a good range of Robinson's beers.

What to see

In Mosedale you'll see the tiny burial ground associated with the Friends Meeting House. George Fox, founder of the Society of Friends, came to speak in Mosedale in 1653, and soon after there was an established meeting of local Quakers. There are no headstones in the burial ground, following the Quaker tradition, but the last interment was in 1921 and the site is no longer used for burial. The simple meeting house is up the lane on the left. It was built in 1702 and carefully restored by volunteers in the 1970s. Meetings are still held there today and in the summer months it houses a coffee shop.

GLENDERAMACKIN AND SOUTHER FELL

DISTANCE/TIME	5.25 miles (8.4km) / 3hrs
ASCENT/GRADIENT	985ft (300m) / ▲ ▲ ▲
PATHS	Grassy and stony paths, open fellside
LANDSCAPE	Remote river valley, open exposed fellside
SUGGESTED MAP	OS Explorer OL5 The English Lakes (NE)
START/FINISH	Grid reference: NY364302
DOG FRIENDLINESS	Under control at all times; whole area grazed by sheep
PARKING	Car park opposite village hall (with honesty box)
PUBLIC TOILETS	None on route

With an air of the theatrical, the little River Glenderamackin weaves a circuitous course around Souther (pronounced sue-ter) Fell, passing through, on its meanderings, the little hamlet of Mungrisdale (pronounced mun-grize-dale). Whereas the central Lakeland fells are composed of hard volcanic rocks, Souther Fell and its neighbouring hills are made up of the relatively soft rocks of Skiddaw slate. The resultant smooth and rounded terrain of this mountain region gives an air of wild desolation. On this walk, a long gradual ascent following the river provides an easy way to climb Souther Fell. The rewards, once the heights are crested, are expansive views east over the plains of the Eden Valley, and behind to the dark crags and combes of Bannerdale Crags and the great Blencathra mountain.

The majority of place-names in these parts are Celtic; Mungo (a Celtic missionary), Blencathra and Glenderamackin are typical examples. Indeed, the remains of an important Celtic hill-fort still form a defensive ring around the nearby summit of Carrock Fell just to the north, and it is thought that northern Cumbria was still part of the Kingdom of Strathclyde in the 10th century.

Phantom army

Locals have long said that a ghostly army of warriors marches over Souther Fell on Midsummer's Eve, a legend that goes back to 1745, the year Bonnie Prince Charlie returned to march on England. Following reports that both soldiers and horsemen had been seen marching along the high shoulder of Souther Fell, a group of 26 local men stationed themselves at a suitable vantage point in the valley below on the evening before midsummer, determined to put to rest the rumours and speculation. To their incredulity they witnessed a rapidly moving line of troops, horses and carriages. The line spread right across the high summit shoulder of the fell in a continuous chain. Steep places and rocky outcrops neither slowed nor disrupted progress of this huge army. They couldn't believe their eyes – yet only darkness put an effective end to these strange events. The next day there was nothing to be seen so, with considerable trepidation, half-expecting that the invasion from over the border had begun, a party climbed to the summit – where they found nothing. Not a mark in the grass, no footprint, hoof-print or wheel rut, and of an army there was not the remotest sign. So convinced were the 26 men, and determined that their integrity should be respected, that they all swore an oath before a magistrate as to what they had seen. It remains a mystery, yet Bonnie Prince Charlie was to invade in the November of that same year.

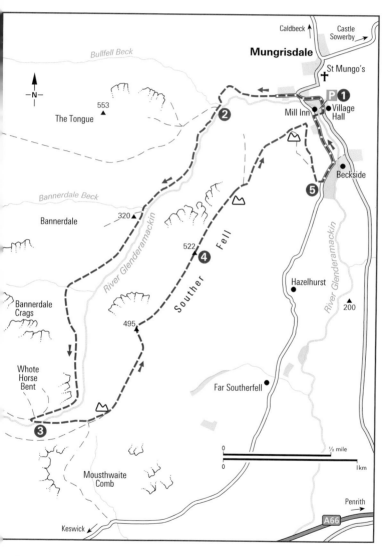

1. With your back to the parking area, turn left along the road, following the River Glenderamackin upstream. After passing a lane to the Mill Inn on the left, go left, past a red telephone kiosk, to follow a little lane between the cottages. Continue along the rough track above the north bank of the river. Follow the

footpath as it bends away from the river and passes through a boggy area on a path of slate slabs before returning to cross Bullfell Beck on a footbridge.

2. A few paces beyond Bullfell Beck, as the main track starts to climb steeply, bear left along a lesser path that traces a route along the west bank of the Glenderamackin. The going is straightforward, although the path has been eroded in places and there is a steep drop down to the little river. Continue along the track, boggy in places, to ford Bannerdale Beck. Continue above a fenced area of tree-planting and round the shoulder of Bannerdale Crags, intriguingly named White Horse Bent by the Ordnance Survey. Continue the ascent until a narrow trail drops left to a footbridge to cross the River Glenderamackin, which is hardly 6ft (2m) wide at this point.

3. Follow the path (with frequent glances back at the dramatic form of Blencathra) as it ascends diagonally left to a high grassy saddle. Bear left, following the path and ascend the long shoulder of Souther Fell. In a slight dip, fork left to a prominent cairn for a superb view of Blencathra and Bannerdale Crags. Bear right back to the main path and continue, through another gentle dip, to a rise capped by a few rocks: the summit.

4. Keep north and continue to descend the grassy nose of the fell. Easy at first, the angle steepens progressively. Follow the path carefully to negotiate a little crag. A few dozen strides after this rocky section, and just before a gap through another area of bare rock, bear right at a faint fork in the path. A trail, obscured in summer by high bracken, slants down right towards a clump of tall conifers. Continue beside a fence until it meets a road near the trees.

5. Go left down the road, through a gate, until you reach the Mill Inn's car park. Immediately take the signposted path to the right that drops to cross another relatively new bridge over the Glenderamackin. The car park where the walk started is now on the left.

Where to eat and drink
The Mill Inn at Mungrisdale dates from the 16th century and offers bar meals and a choice of real ales. Children and dogs are welcome, and there is a garden to relax in during the summer months.

What to see
Sited next to the road in Mungrisdale and worth inspection is another charming little church that takes its name from St Kentigern (or St Mungo, meaning 'the loved one'). St Mungo, later Bishop of Glasgow, is thought to have been a missionary from Ireland who preached at a number of churches in Cumbria some time around the 6th century.

While you're there
For solitude and contemplation there are few more rewarding places to visit than another tiny church of St Kentigern (or St Mungo) at Castle Sowerby. It's not easy to find, but the views of the fells from here are sublime.

LOUGHRIGG FELL FROM AMBLESIDE

DISTANCE/TIME	3.25 miles (5.3km) / 1hr 45min
ASCENT/GRADIENT	575ft (175m) / ▲ ▲ ▲
PATHS	Road, paths and tracks, can be muddy in places, several stiles
LANDSCAPE	Town, park and open hillside with views to high fells
SUGGESTED MAP	OS Explorer OL7 The English Lakes (SE)
START/FINISH	Grid reference: NY375047
DOG FRIENDLINESS	Under control; busy roads, park, sheep grazing
PARKING	Ambleside central car park
PUBLIC TOILETS	At car park

Loughrigg is a delightful low fell, running from Ambleside and the head of Windermere lake towards both Langdale and Grasmere. This walk crosses the River Rothay by Miller Bridge, and rises to a craggy viewpoint before traversing the small Lily Tarn, to return via the stone lane of Miller Brow. With the exception of possibly thick mist or cloud, this is a walk for all seasons and most weather conditions. The views, south over Waterhead and down Windermere and north over the wooded vale of Rydal into the high mountain drama of the Fairfield Horseshoe, are some of the most evocative in the region. The delightful detail of tree, rocky knoll, heather, bracken and the white and green cup and saucers of the lilies on Lily Tarn contrast with the grand open views of mountain, dale and lake.

Ambleside

Even before the heights of lovely Loughrigg are reached, the varied slate stone buildings of Ambleside provide an intriguing start to the walk. There is a lot more to this little town than just being the outdoor equipment capital of Britain. Sited in the old county of Westmorland, Ambleside has been occupied for a long time – Bronze Age remains, c.2000 BC, can be seen on the nearby fells, and the Galava Roman fort near Waterhead was one of the most important in northwest England. How Head, just up the Kirkstone road, is one of the oldest surviving buildings in old Ambleside, located in the area known as Above Stock. Sections of this fine stone house date back to the 16th century, and it was once the lodge of the Master Forester of the Barony of Kendal. It has massive circular chimneys – a typical Westmorland feature – and stone mullioned windows, and incorporates stone from the old Roman fort at Waterhead and cobbles from the bed of Stock Ghyll Beck.

Stock Ghyll once served as the heartbeat of the town when, some 150 years ago, it provided water power for 12 watermills. This walk passes a restored waterwheel, immediately followed by the famous Bridge House, one of the most photographed buildings in the Lake District. Spanning the beck, this tiny 17th-century building is said to have been built this way to avoid paying land tax. Locally it is said to have once housed a family with six children. It is now a shop and information centre for the National Trust. Ambleside has become a major tourist resort with shops, hotels and restaurants, and is a convenient base for exploring the rest of the Lake District.

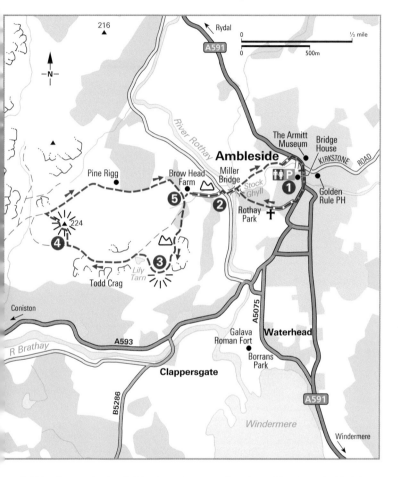

1. Take the wooden footbridge from the car park and go right, along the Rydal road, to pass the waterwheel and Bridge House. At the junction bear right down Compston Road. At the next junction, by the cinema, turn right then immediately left to enter Vicarage Road. Pass between church and school to enter Rothay Park. Follow the main path through the park, then cross a flat bridge over Stock Ghyll beck. Go left to cross the stone-arched Miller Bridge spanning the River Rothay.

2. Turn right, cross a cattle grid, then climb a steep road on the left, which becomes rougher by the buildings of Brow Head Farm. At the S-bend just above, a stone stile leads up and left. Walk through trees to a little bridge. Cross and climb steps, then bear left at a fork. Slant across a wooded slope,

then ascend a little valley. At a junction turn left. The path makes a rising traverse then swings right and climbs near a wall. Cross a ladder stile and climb a rocky knoll offering definitive views of the Fairfield Horseshoe to the north and Windermere to the south.

3. The way descends to the right to join a well-defined path. Follow this to pass a little pond before cresting a rise and falling to lovely little Lily Tarn. The path skirts the right edge of the tarn, then roughly follows the crest of the fell before joining a wall on the left. Follow this down through a kissing gate and climb the broad knoll ahead, another worthy viewpoint.

4. Take the path descending right to a prominent track below. Turn right along the track to a gate that leads through the stone wall boundary of the open fell and into a field. Continue down, passing a striking house at Pine Rigg, on the site of the old golf clubhouse. Intercept the original route just above the buildings of Brow Head.

5. Continue to cross Miller Bridge, then go straight ahead through an iron gate. Follow the track through fields. A short street leads to the main Rydal road. Bear right on the road to the car park beyond the fire station.

Where to eat and drink

There are many places to eat and drink in Ambleside: inns, cafes and restaurants abound in the town. Try the Golden Rule pub, on Smithy Brow, a traditional pub with a friendly atmosphere.

What to see

Lily Tarn, just after Point 3, is naturally known for its white water-lilies. The lilies have lightly scented white flowers that unfurl between June and September. Despite its great beauty it has a sinister reputation; while its blooms may tempt the inquisitive, rope-like stems that grow up to 8ft (2.4m) long can easily ensnare the unwary.

While you're there

The Armitt Museum, opposite the car park, provides a fascinating look at Ambleside and its environs in times past. An area is devoted to children's author and illustrator Beatrix Potter, where her desk and some of her natural history watercolours are on display. Borrans Park at Waterhead (with Galava Roman Fort next to it) and Rothay Park both provide pleasant recreational areas for those with a little time to spare, the latter having an excellent children's play area.

18

SATTERTHWAITE AND RUSLAND WOODLANDS

DISTANCE/TIME	4.4 miles (7.15km) / 2hrs
ASCENT/GRADIENT	940ft (287m) / ▲ ▲
PATHS	Mainly good paths and tracks throughout
LANDSCAPE	Gentle hills cloaked in mixed woodland and forest
SUGGESTED MAP	OS Explorer OL7 The English Lakes (SE)
START/FINISH	Grid reference: SD344912
DOG FRIENDLINESS	Use lead for roads and farmland
PARKING	Forest car park at Blind Lane
PUBLIC TOILETS	None on route

Although a serenely peaceful place today, it is not long since this forest and the streams that course through it supported a range of industries, many of which had operated for centuries. Little more than 100 years ago, you would still have been able to find working watermills in the valleys and see woodcutters at work coppicing the trees. The air was once heavy with the smoke of charcoal burning or the acrid smell of iron smelting. Strange as it may seem, if it had not been for that industrial tradition, the rich forests and woodlands that today lend so much character and beauty to this corner of Lakeland might have disappeared long ago, replaced by the open sheep walks prevalent throughout so much of the countryside.

Medieval industry

Before the Dissolution of the Monasteries, the monks at Furness Abbey managed extensive iron ore mines and needed a constant supply of charcoal to reduce it to iron. The woodland here provided a ready source of timber, but simply to fell the trees would have exhausted the stock before a new crop could be grown. However, by coppicing the boles a steady supply of small timber was guaranteed, since new wood could be harvested every 15 years or so. Bloomeries (small furnaces) were established deep within the forest, for it was more economic to bring in the ore than take out the charcoal. After the monks were expelled, the estates passed into private hands and the industries continued to grow. By the 18th century new techniques needed power to drive machinery. Mills sprang up beside the streams, powering bellows and forge hammers that beat impurities from the metal, which was being produced in ever-larger and more efficient furnaces around Backbarrow. This walk passes two former mills – Force Forge and Force Mills.

Rich habitat

Although the industry here has now disappeared, the forest remains an important resource, managed to provide a renewable supply of timber for today's manufacturers. It is also a rich wildlife habitat, and valued as a recreational retreat. In many ways, the forest is being made to work just as hard today as it has ever done, and long may it remain for future generations to enjoy.

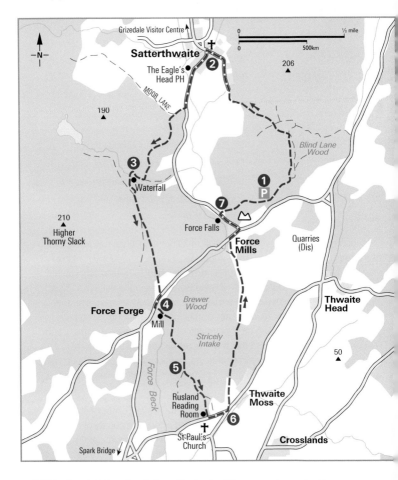

1. Take the right-hand path from the back of the car park, marked by green-and white-topped posts, heading over a rise to a forest track. Turn left and, after 400yds (366m), turn left on a steep path through birch trees. Cross another track at the top and descend. At the bottom bear right on a metalled track into Satterthwaite.

2. Turn left by the church and walk through the village. After 0.25 miles (400m), at a left-hand bend, go right onto a track, Moor Lane, and shortly bear left on a path rising into the trees. Fork left at a post. The path goes through a dry-stone wall sculpture, descends across a vague track, then meets a clearer one.

3. Turn right. Passing a waterfall, look out for *Bathers*, part of the forest art project (see walk 19). The track bends across the stream and rises to a

junction. Turn left for 220yds (201m) and branch left again onto an unmarked and inconspicuous, descending footpath.

4. Emerging onto a lane at the bottom, go right, then turn left between cottages at Force Forge. Cross a stile on the right, in front of a house, then follow a tall beech hedge round left to a bridge. Continue through a deer fence into Brewer Wood, then turn right on a wider track.

5. Go through another deer fence. Eventually fork left (waymarked) and carry on through trees. At an indistinct fork beyond the crest of the hill, take the right-hand branch, which descends to the Rusland Reading Room. Cross a stile and walk out to the lane by St Paul's church. Turn left. (If you miss the indistinct fork, don't worry, as the left branch also leads to the church.)

6. Soon leave the lane for a byway opposite a junction. Climb beside wooded pastures, then drop to a lane at Force Mills. Go right and then left to ascend beside Force Falls.

7. At a green and white post, part-way up the hill, turn right onto a path climbing steeply into a larch plantation. Turn right and climb to a gap in a wall. A little further on, bear right (green waymark) and descend back to the car park.

Where to eat and drink

The route passes The Eagle's Head at Satterthwaite. It's a friendly, welcoming pub serving Theakston's ales and tasty bar meals, but it's not normally open weekday lunchtimes. There's also a café at Grizedale Visitor Centre, higher up the valley.

What to see

In a quiet corner of St Paul's churchyard in Rusland lie the ashes of Arthur Ransome (1884–1967), loved by many for his wonderful children's stories. He spent his childhood holidays at High Nibthwaite on Coniston Water and developed a lifelong passion for the area. Ransome worked for much of his life as a journalist, but came to live in the Lakes in 1925, where he wrote *Swallows and Amazons* and several other books.

While you're there

Coppiced wood was used for a wide assortment of products, including barrels, baskets, hurdles and tanning bark. Another important industry was bobbin manufacturing, supplying the Pennine spinning and weaving sheds, which used them by the million. Nearby Stott Park Bobbin Mill operated from 1835 to 1971 and is now a working museum, where you can step back in time to see bobbins made just as they were in Queen Victoria's day.

19

GRIZEDALE FOREST TRAILS

DISTANCE/TIME	6.4 miles (10.3km) / 3hrs
ASCENT/GRADIENT	1,160ft (353m) / ▲ ▲
PATHS	Forest tracks and woodland paths
LANDSCAPE	Conifer plantations and mixed woodland
SUGGESTED MAP	OS Explorer OL7 The English Lakes (SE)
START/FINISH	Grid reference: SD336944
DOG FRIENDLINESS	Most of the route is shared use, with many cyclists around. Keep dogs under close control
PARKING	Large car park just south of Visitor Centre
PUBLIC TOILETS	At Visitor Centre

Grizedale has always been at least partly forested, from the time when wild boar were hunted here by Norman barons to the present day, when 6,047 acres (2,447ha) are covered, mainly with conifers. Perhaps the guilt of planting all those gloomy Christmas trees got too much for the foresters in the 1970s – it was then that the 'art in the park' idea was born. There are now more than 60 permanent sculptures dotted around the forest. Round one corner there may be a wolf; round the next there's something that you can't quite comprehend, perhaps waiting for you to give it meaning. Some works, especially those made from natural materials, weather and change over time; and sometimes other things change around them. A good example is the large wood-carved ring that you'll see on the descent from Carron Crag. This is *17 Degrees South* by Linda Watson. Originally it created a perfect frame for the view down to the village of Satterthwaite; now, however, the trees have grown too tall.

Another aspect of the forest which you're bound to observe is its immense popularity for cycling and mountain biking. The forest roads cater for all abilities, while more hardcore mountain bikers take to purpose-built trails and the bridleways and byways that cut across the forest. After Carron Crag you'll have several glimpses of the North Face Trail, especially as you descend from the turning circle (Point 4). This red-graded route (mountain bike trails are often graded in order of difficulty, like ski runs, green, blue, red and black) attracts a range of abilities and this is its main climb.

Silurian story

The route follows the green waymarks of the Silurian Trail almost to Satterthwaite, taking in the summit of Carron Crag, the best viewpoint of the day. To the west the Coniston fells are laid out across the horizon, and to the south Morecambe Bay is a shimmering presence. And all around – you'll have scrambled up them to reach the trig point – are the Silurian rocks of the Windermere Supergroup, which give the trail its name. They may be a little younger than the rocks of the high fells – a mere 425 million years old – but these slates and mudstones still have plenty of character.

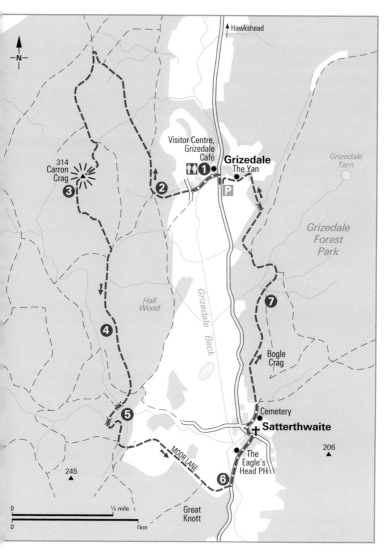

1. With your back to the café, go under the arch by the shop, out to a lane and turn right. After crossing a stream, the bike routes go left on a track. Go straight ahead up a waymarked path with a few steps. The path leaves and recrosses a bridleway before reaching a forestry road, where you turn right.

2. Pass another bridleway, then the exit of the black bike route, before forking left up a stony track with green and red waymarks, climbing steadily. After dipping to ford a couple of streams, a narrow path on the left cuts across to a forestry road just above. Turn left and follow the road south. Keep left then, where the track bends sharp left, go straight ahead on a path which wriggles through trees and scrub to the summit trig point.

3. The path descends to rejoin the forestry road. Turn right to a crossroads of tracks, where you go straight ahead (south). The track ends at a turning circle.

4. The North Face Trail comes up from the right while our route continues straight ahead as a narrow path that weaves through lovely mixed woodland. Along this section you'll see a series of symbolic art sculptures. Cross the North Face Trail and descend to a forestry road. Turn right, then keep left down into the gill. Fork left before the main track crosses a bridge.

5. Follow the path over two stone bridges. Where it rejoins the track, go right a few paces then left up a waymarked path, passing a shelter before meeting the track again. Cross at an angle, following green posts, descend and turn left on another track. Leaving the forest, the track becomes a narrow walled lane, Moor Lane, dropping to the Satterthwaite road at a small car park.

6. Turn left along the lane into Satterthwaite, passing The Eagle's Head. Bear right after the church, then turn right on a steep lane, which climbs past the cemetery. At the terminus take the left of two lilac-banded waymarks, the Bogle Crag Trail. The path heads north through woodland, traversing wooded slopes. Ignoring paths climbing on the right, continue to a forest road and turn right.

7. At the next junction, go left (really straight ahead) on a winding forestry trail. Abandon this at a white waymark for a path on the left. Make a winding descent, following signs for Visitor Centre, then join a tarmac track. Keep left at a fork, pass beneath a footbridge, then double back left and follow the path past the striking Yan building and the terraces of the old hall to the car park.

Where to eat and drink
The Grizedale Café at the Grizedale Visitor Centre serves food to either take away or eat in, with outdoor seating for sunny days. Hearty pies and quiches are a speciality. The walk also passes The Eagle's Head at Satterthwaite.

What to see
The ancient oak woods around Bogle Crag once provided the charcoal needed for iron smelting. You may notice the old flattened hollows of the charcoal pitsteads. You will also see a restored potash pit beside the Bogle Crag Trail.

While you're there
Children's author Beatrix Potter has connections with this area. Her farm at Hill Top, Near Sawrey, which she bought with the royalties of her first book, *The Tale of Peter Rabbit* (1900), is full of Potter memorabilia. The National Trust's Beatrix Potter Gallery at Hawkshead displays many of her original illustrations.

20

AROUND RYDAL WATER

DISTANCE/TIME	3 miles (4.8km) / 1hr 30min
ASCENT/GRADIENT	460ft (140m) / ▲
PATHS	Stony paths and tracks
LANDSCAPE	Rydal Water nestling in wooded vale below high fells
SUGGESTED MAP	OS Explorer OL7 The English Lakes (SE)
START/FINISH	Grid reference: NY348066
DOG FRIENDLINESS	Generally suitable for dogs; grazing sheep, 2 road crossings
PARKING	Car parks either side of A591 at White Moss Common
PUBLIC TOILETS	Below the A591, between the two car parks

This classic walk of breathtaking beauty will surely be forever associated with the poet William Wordsworth (1770–1850). From all around the world people come here to see the landscape that so inspired him. His poetry broke with the conventional structure and stylised imagery of his day to explore nature and human emotion in a new poetic language. He lived at Dove Cottage – close by in Grasmere – between 1799 and 1808, and at Rydal Mount (passed on this walk) from 1813 until his death. Although Rydal Mount was his home for a much longer period, the Dove Cottage years are often seen as the most creative part of his life. Wordsworth's sister Dorothy (1771–1855) lived with the poet throughout his life, often sharing in long walks which were an integral part of their life. They thought little of walking to Keswick and back to visit friends like fellow poet Robert Southey. Dorothy's own literary output was largely disregarded during her lifetime, but her *Grasmere Journal*, first published in 1897, shows her to have been a perceptive observer and accomplished writer. Many now believe that Wordsworth's output owes much to her keen eye and turn of phrase.

Familiar walk
This little circuit of Rydal Water would have been deeply familiar to both Wordsworths and they would still recognise most of it today, though they might be horrified by the roar of traffic on the A591 and shocked by the sheer popularity of the paths through the woods and along Loughrigg Terrace. The best place to get a sense of the landscape that they knew is probably in the later stages, as you climb past Rydal Mount and then traverse the hillside along the old Coffin Route. Despite its popularity, this outing can never fail to inspire. Each season is different. Whether the lake is clad in ice, or the flora in springtime blossom, it is a landscape to lift the spirit. This walk, with a little ascent and descent, visits wood, lake and river. Dippers can often be seen on the river, swans on the lake, ravens on Nab Scar, and roe deer in the woods.

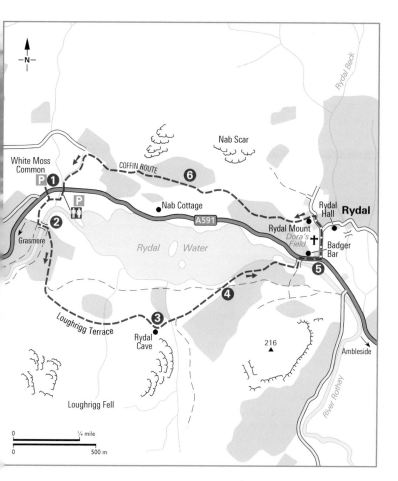

1. From the entrance to the higher car park, cross the road, descend steps and bear right to join a wide track near picnic tables. (From the lower car park, pass a low barrier and 'White Moss Walks' board). Follow the track over a footbridge.

2. Ascend, forking right near the top, to a gate leading to a stony track. Take the path ahead, slanting left and up through the bracken to a level path known as Loughrigg Terrace. Traverse left along the path, with fine views over the lake to Nab Cottage and Nab Scar. Continue along the path, rising slightly around a shoulder to a level area of slate waste. On the right is the entrance to Rydal Cave, an old slate quarry.

3. Take the track directly below the cave, descending through a larch wood and past another quarry hole and caves. Keep along the track, which soon descends between stone walls. Continue to a signpost, turn sharp left, then back right to enter woods by a gate just above the shore of Rydal Water.

4. The path leads through the wood and then across a pasture to a bridge over the River Rothay. Cross the bridge, which leads to the A591; the Badger Bar

stands opposite. Cross the road and turn right. Soon you reach a lane that leads uphill to the left.

5. Follow the lane up past Rydal church and Dora's Field, then climb more steeply still to Rydal Mount. Immediately below the house, a track goes left, signed 'Public Bridleway Grasmere'. Follow this track, the old Coffin Route between Ambleside and Grasmere. Stony in places, the track is well defined, traversing clumps of oaks with a view over Rydal Water. After a more open stretch, the track enters the woods above Nab Cottage.

6. Keep along the track through some stony dips and rises; there is never any doubt of the route. Unusual retaining walls just above on one stretch are an exposed part of the Thirlmere Aqueduct, which conveys the waters of that lake all the way to Manchester. After a short, rocky descent, the track reaches a gate below a house on the right. Go through the gate, and in a few more paces turn left on a steep path down the hillside. Continue down through the wood to meet the A591 just above the lower car park at White Moss Common; the higher car park is just to the right.

Where to eat and drink
The Badger Bar at Rydal offers bar meals and a pleasant beer garden, ideal to relax in on a hot summer's afternoon. Otherwise, it's only a short way up the road to Grasmere, with its wide choice of pubs, cafés and restaurants.

What to see
Rydal Mount was the last home of William Wordsworth. Open to the public, the house, with its family portraits, furniture and some of the poet's personal possessions, is set in exquisite gardens, designed by Wordsworth himself. Rented from Lady Diana le Fleming, who lived in Rydal Hall, it was home to William, his wife and family and to his sister Dorothy.

While you're there
Rydal church, partly designed by William Wordsworth, is worthy of closer inspection. Behind the church is Dora's Field, with its stand of oaks and pines, full of golden daffodils between late March and early April. This piece of steeply dipping hillside beneath Rydal Mount was dedicated by William Wordsworth to his daughter Dora, to whom he was very close and who died of tuberculosis aged 42.

ALCOCK TARN

21

DISTANCE/TIME	3 miles (4.8km) / 2hrs 15min
ASCENT/GRADIENT	984ft (300m) / ▲ ▲ ▲
PATHS	Road, grassy paths and tracks
LANDSCAPE	Woods, field, fell, tarn and lake
SUGGESTED MAP	OS Explorer OL7 The English Lakes (SE)
START/FINISH	Grid reference: NY339073
DOG FRIENDLINESS	Some places grazed by sheep
PARKING	National Park Authority Stock Lane pay-and-display car park, on the southern side of Grasmere village
PUBLIC TOILETS	At car park

The name 'Dove Cottage' would not have meant anything to William Wordsworth and his family. The little house beneath the woods and towering ridge of Heron Pike was known to the poet and his family as Town End and it had formerly been an ale house called the Dove and Olive Bough. The Wordsworths arrived there on foot, just before Christmas in the winter of 1799. They paid £8 a year in rent and left nine years later for a variety of homes before ending up a few miles away at Rydal in 1813. William described it as their 'beautiful and quiet home'.

Dove Cottage today is a whole complex of academic and artistic endeavours as well as a museum and art gallery. This walk ends by the Jerwood Centre, opened by poet Seamus Heaney. It houses an academic reading room for the Wordsworth Trust's collection of historic manuscripts. It's fair to say that the Wordsworths would probably not realise this was the same place that William settled in to write 'Daffodils', and his sister Dorothy her diaries of their time there. Some things may be familiar though. The mercilessly steep section of this walk that leads from the back of Forest Side and takes you up into Greenhead Gill is still perhaps as stiff a climb as Wordsworth described it in 'Michael':

> *If from the public way you turn your steps,*
> *Up the tumultuous brook of Greenhead Ghyll,*
> *You will suppose that with an upright path,*
> *Your feet must struggle in such bold ascent,*
> *The pastoral mountains front you, face to face*
> *But courage! for around that boisterous brook*
> *The mountains have all opened out themselves*
> *And made a hidden valley of their own.*

Missing from the gill in Wordsworth's day would be the parapet of the Thirlmere Aqueduct and associated pieces of water supply equipment.

Alcock Tarn

Another addition since 'Michael' would be the tarn in the hollow beneath Butter Crag. Alcock Tarn was once a boggy depression and took its name from the rocks that rise above on the slopes of Heron Pike. Mr Alcock of the Hollins in the valley below enlarged it with a dam and stocked it with trout at the end of the 19th century. Alcock Tarn was bought, along with much of the surrounding fell, by the National Trust in the 1940s.

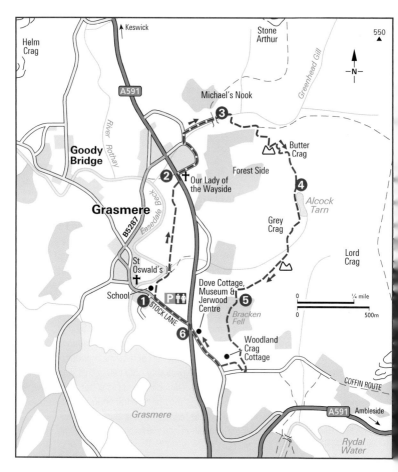

1. From the far end of the car park, close to the toilets, locate a walled path passing the back of Grasmere School. Turn right at a junction and pass the old Workman's Reading Room. Keep ahead at a crossing of paths by a small bridge and go through a kissing gate to join a meadow path. It bears left by a stand of pines then follows a wall and fences to reach the main road.

2. Turn left along the pavement for a few paces before crossing over to the lane adjacent to the Catholic church. Walk up this quiet residential lane. At a junction after a short descent, turn right and continue until a footpath sign on the right points you up a narrower walled lane towards Alcock Tarn. At the top of this lane, go through a gate onto the open fell.

3. Turn immediately right. Walk up the right-hand side of the beck as you look up. The path ascends steeply alongside, following the wall away from the beck then cutting up past a bench before rejoining the wall. Keep climbing; there's a very brief respite near the corner of another wall before you continue zig-zagging up the hill. A line of crags fills your immediate horizon until you work your way beyond them, swinging round to the right and levelling off. Continue on the well-walked route. A wall joins you on one side and a gate takes you through a crossing wall to Alcock Tarn.

4. Half-way along, a little bluff on the right affords great views of the valley below. Pass the tarn and its dam and bear right, aiming for a gap in the wall. A way now descends beside the rocky promontory of Grey Crag, a zig-zag path beginning just beneath the crag itself. The descent is steep and rocky in places but navigation is fairly straightforward, following a clear path down to a gate. Through this the descent continues past a bench and a tiny reservoir under trees. At a junction of tracks, keep left on a wider path. Go through a metal gate into shady woods and continue to a second gate.

5. Keep ahead around the grounds of Wood Close, descending to a lane. Don't go out onto the lane, but turn right, descending on a footpath that emerges at Woodland Crag Cottage. Turn left along the access road and left again on a tarmac lane. After a few paces a right-hand dodge cuts off the corner down to a road. Turn right here, by a coffin resting stone. Emerge at Dove Cottage, walking past the museum and gallery to the main road.

6. Turn right to cross beyond the mini-roundabout, then follow Stock Lane back toward Grasmere and the car park.

Where to eat and drink

The café at Dove Cottage is open seven days a week and open to all. Alcock Tarn is a perfect place for a picnic, and there are plenty of other options, from straightforward cafés to expensive restaurants, in Grasmere village beyond the car park.

What to see

The little flourish of crag that marks your descent route is known as Grey Crag. It is the principal destination of the Guides Race at the annual Grasmere Sports, held late August, the runners taking the direct route from the sports field up the steep field below the fell and back again. The record for the seniors' race is just over 12 minutes!

While you're there

Take a bit more time to visit Dove Cottage and the Wordsworth Museum. It's packed full of contemporary exhibits that put the poet and his group of friends and family in context. When you've finished here, you can wander into Grasmere village and see his grave in St Oswald's churchyard.

WALKING BY ELTER WATER AND LOUGHRIGG TARN

22

DISTANCE/TIME	4 miles (6.4km) / 2hrs
ASCENT/GRADIENT	328ft (100m) / ▲ ▲
PATHS	Grassy and stony paths and tracks, surfaced lane, several stiles
LANDSCAPE	Lake, tarn, fields, woods, open fellside, views to fells
SUGGESTED MAP	OS Explorer OL7 The English Lakes (SE)
START/FINISH	Grid reference: NY328048
DOG FRIENDLINESS	Under control at all times; fellside grazed by sheep
PARKING	National Trust pay-and-display car park at Elterwater village
PUBLIC TOILETS	Above car park in Elterwater village

Although it does include steep sections of ascent and descent, this is not a particularly difficult walk, and there are outstanding views throughout. The little lake of Elter Water and the petite Loughrigg Tarn are among the prettiest stretches of water in the region. The former, really three interconnected basins, was originally named Eltermere, which translates directly from the Old Norse into 'swan lake'. The swans are still here in abundance; if you eat your lunch sitting on the wooden bench at the foot of the lake, be careful they don't grab your sandwiches. The views over both lake and tarn, to the reclining lion profile of the Langdale Pikes, are particularly evocative. Each season paints a different picture: golden daffodils by Langdale Beck in early spring; bluebells in Rob Rash woods in May; yellow maple in Elterwater village in October; and a thousand shades of green, everywhere, all summer. The river is dominant throughout the lower stages of the walk. It starts as the Great Langdale Beck, before emerging from the confines of Elter Water as the sedate River Brathay. Ascent then leads to the suspended bowl of Loughrigg Tarn, followed by the open fell freedom of Little Loughrigg. This is very much a walk for all seasons, and should the section through the meadows by the Brathay be flooded, then a simple detour can easily be made onto the road to bypass the problem.

Local gunpowder works

With all the quarrying and mining that once took place in the Lake District, including a little poaching for the pot, there used to be a considerable demand for 'black powder' or gunpowder. Elterwater Gunpowder Works, founded in 1824, once filled that demand. The natural water power of Langdale Beck was utilised to drive great grinding wheels or millstones. Prime-quality charcoal came from the local coppices, while saltpetre and sulphur were imported. In the 1890s the works employed around 80 people. Accidental explosions did occur, notably in 1916, when four men were killed. The whole enterprise closed down in 1929. Today the site is occupied by the Langdale Timeshare organisation, with only the massive mill wheels on display to bear witness to times past. While the works were operational, the raw ingredients were brought in and the highly explosive gunpowder taken away by horse and cart. Clydesdales were preferred for their huge strength and considerable intelligence. On workdays they would be harnessed up, and on special occasions they had their manes plaited and ribboned, and were decorated with polished horse brasses. The horses have long gone, but some of their brasses remain fixed to the oak beams in the Brittania Inn.

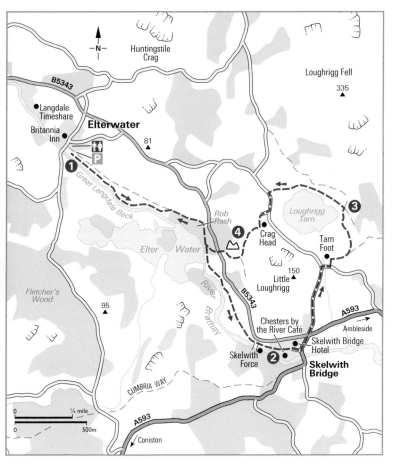

1. Pass through a small gate to walk downstream above Great Langdale Beck. Continue into the woods of Rob Rash. A gate leads through the stone wall; the open foot of Elter Water lies to the right. Continue along the path through the meadows above the river. Note that this section can be wet and is prone to occasional flooding. Pass through the gate and enter woods. Pass a footbridge over the river, then pass Skelwith Force waterfall down to the right. Steps and metal bridges lead to a viewing point above the falls. Keep along the path to pass through industrial buildings formerly belonging to Kirkstone Quarry.

2. Chesters by the River café is on the right as the path becomes a small surfaced road. Continue ahead to meet the A593 by the bridge over the river, where there are picnic benches. Turn left to pass the hotel. At the road junction, cross the Great Langdale road to climb a steep, narrow lane. At a T-junction turn right over a bridge then left on a rocky track, which becomes a narrow path. Joining a track, turn left then fork right, passing in front of cottages. At a junction go left and then through the left-hand one of two gates. Follow the level track to overlook Loughrigg Tarn. Part-way along the tarn, cross a stile over the railings on the left.

3. Walk down the meadow to traverse just above the tarn, with the water on your left. The footpath swings left to climb a ladder stile over a wall. Follow the grassy track uphill to join the road. Turn left and continue until a surfaced drive leads right, signed 'Public Footpath Skelwith Bridge'. Pass a small cottage; the track ends at a higher cottage, Crag Head. Go straight ahead on a stony path and in a few paces turn right on a narrow grassy path climbing steeply up the hillside, to gain a level shoulder on Little Loughrigg.

4. Cross the shoulder and descend the path, keeping right at forks, to meet a stone wall. Descend near the wall to find, in a few hundred yards, a gate into the upper woods of Rob Rash. A steep descent leads down to the road. Go straight across, and descend a track to meet up with the outward route. Bear right to return to Elterwater village.

Where to eat and drink

The popular Britannia Inn, in the centre of the Elterwater village, serves real ales and bar meals year-round. En route, Chesters by the River Café offers vegetarian fare of high quality. Its takeaway annexe, with outside seating, is handy when the main café's full. The Skelwith Bridge Hotel also offers bar meals.

What to see

Carrying the full contents of the River Brathay over a vertical drop of some 30ft (9m), Skelwith Force waterfall is an impressive sight. A little bridge provides access to the rocks above the force, and steps and a walkway lead to lower rocks and a good viewpoint. Access is unrestricted, though the rocks are polished and the waterfall unguarded. A weir once diverted water from above the falls to power the mills at Skelwith Bridge just downstream.

While you're there

It's well worth heading further up the B5343 into Great Langdale. There are impressive views of the Langdale Pikes, Bowfell and Crinkle Crags. The area is also an important neolithic site; there was a stone-axe 'factory' high on the slopes of Pike o'Stickle. Much closer to the road, the Langdale Boulders at Copt Howe have two panels of ancient cup and ring markings, discovered in 1999.

HODGE CLOSE AND LITTLE LANGDALE

DISTANCE/TIME	4.5 miles (7.2km) / 2hrs
ASCENT/GRADIENT	623ft (190m) / ▲
PATHS	Stony paths and tracks, road
LANDSCAPE	Disused slate quarries, village below high fells, wooded dales, river
SUGGESTED MAP	OS Explorer OL7 The English Lakes (SE)
START/FINISH	Grid reference: NY316017
DOG FRIENDLINESS	Generally good; sheep grazing and short road section
PARKING	On Hodge Close Quarry Bank by roadside
PUBLIC TOILETS	None on route

From Yewdale, the quiet vale of Tilberthwaite corkscrews northwards between brackened and craggy fells into a narrow wooded corridor that reaches the River Brathay in picturesque Little Langdale. A predominance of thick oak and deciduous woods cloak the valley flanks and bottom. Within these woods, old slate quarries litter the landscape, bearing testament to a once prosperous industry. The band of woodland before the descent to Stang End Farm is known locally as Sepulchre Wood and it is said that plague victims who died in Little Langdale were once buried here. After Stang End Farm, the route crosses the River Brathay and soon reaches Little Langdale village, with the Three Shires Inn at its heart. The inn is named after the Three Shires Stone, which stands near the summit of Wrynose Pass, where the old counties of Lancashire, Westmorland and Cumberland met. Leaving the village, the route re-crosses the Brathay by the famous Slater Bridge, which spans the Brathay with two great slabs of slate and a stone arch. It has been speculated that the narrow arch portion of the bridge may be of Roman origin.

Gaping quarries

This walk begins by the gaping hole of Hodge Close Quarry. Extending into Parrock Quarry through a great rock archway, this is reputedly one of the largest artificial holes in England. The quarry, last worked in the early 1970s, is around 100ft (30m) deep, and great caution should be exercised if approaching the edge. Apart from its visible extent, a great water-filled sump leads through tunnels to large underground chambers known as Close Head Quarries. Local folklore tells of Jim Birkett, then apprentice river, or splitter, of the slate, who in the 1930s travelled the length of the quarry hanging by one hand from the jib of an aerial ropeway. Although the edges of the quarry frequently peel away due to the slatey cleavage of the rock, it is a popular recreation area and stones must never be thrown into the workings. Below the rim, often hidden from above, rock climbers scale the walls and divers explore the depths of the deep sump of water.

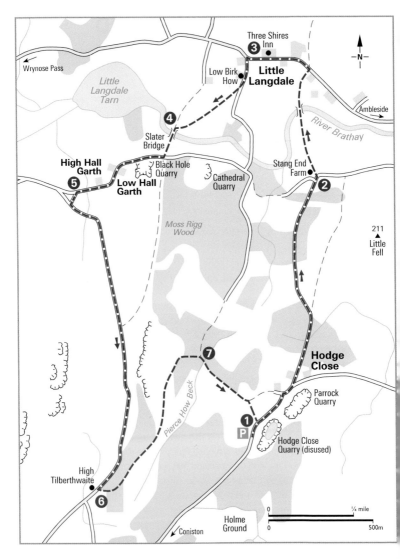

1. From the parking area, follow the road down through the hamlet of Hodge Close and on through a gate. The road continues as a track, though classed as a public road, descending into the woods. Follow the track, past open fields and through more woods before a short descent leads to Stang End Farm.

2. Bear left to find a gate immediately to the left of the first cottage. Pass through the gate, which has a footpath sign, and follow the track down between stone walls. The track opens into a field with a gate and stile. Follow the path bearing right and crossing the field, often flooded, to cross the Lang Parrock footbridge, with steps at both ends, spanning the River Brathay. Ascend the field and take the gate out onto the road. Go left up the road through Little Langdale village to pass the Three Shires Inn.

3. Turn left on a lane signed 'Tilberthwaite. Not recommended for cars'. Pass the white house of Low Birk How to reach steps and a gate on the right. Follow the path up more steps and over the rise to a gate. Follow the narrow path beneath the rocks and through a gap in a stone wall. Descend to a second gap and turn left to Slater Bridge.

4. Cross the bridge and the stile beyond then go up to a gate onto a track. Go right to pass Low Hall Garth and rise steeply past High Hall Garth. The track leads through a gate and fords a stream. Climb more gently to a junction in a few hundred yards; there's a signpost, and Pike o'Stickle appears dramatically beyond the low gap of Blea Tarn.

5. Go sharp left, up the track and over the high shoulder of Knotts. The route is popular with a variety of traffic, including 4x4 off-roaders, and is severely eroded in places, but is always easy to follow. It eventually descends into the farmyard of High Tilberthwaite.

6. Turn sharp left to follow the low-level track back along the valley. The track enters woods, passing cave-like quarry workings and heaps of slate spoil before making a curving descent to the right. At the bottom turn right and continue to cross the stream of Pierce How Beck by a slab bridge.

7. Ascend, passing beneath banks of quarry waste, to a gate. A few paces further on, turn right up steps to a smaller gate. More steps and a steep path over the spoil heap lead directly back to the car park. (If this looks too steep, simply continue up the main track to the hamlet of Hodge Close then turn right to the parking area.)

Where to eat and drink

Passed en route, the Three Shires Inn in Little Langdale offers real ales, bar meals, afternoon teas and ice cream. Post-walk, Coniston is handy and has a good choice of pubs and cafés.

What to see

From the signpost at Point 5, Pike o'Stickle appears dramatically beyond the low gap of Blea Tarn. Looking further left, towards the head of the valley, the last farm is called Fell Foot. Directly behind the farm is a mound, marked on Ordnance Survey maps as Ting Mound, and also known as a Thingmount. This was a place of assembly (thing) for the early Norse settlers.

While you're there

If you turn left instead of right when you meet the track after Slater Bridge, and then climb a gated path on the right after about 200yds (180m), you can find the short tunnel (no torches needed) that leads to the extraordinary underground chamber of Cathedral Quarry. A large 'window' in the rock admits plenty of natural light.

CONISTON TO TARN HOWS

DISTANCE/TIME	6.75 miles (10.9km) / 3hrs 30min
ASCENT/GRADIENT	885ft (270m) / ▲ ▲
PATHS	Road, grassy paths and tracks, several stiles
LANDSCAPE	Woods, field, fell, tarn and lake
SUGGESTED MAP	OS Explorer OL7 The English Lakes (SE)
START/FINISH	Grid reference: SD303975
DOG FRIENDLINESS	Fields grazed by sheep, reasonably suitable for dogs
PARKING	Coniston car park by tourist information centre, or at Sports and Social Club on Shepherds Bridge Lane
PUBLIC TOILETS	At start, and at back of Tarn Hows car park

This long and interesting route contrasts the quiet mixed woods in and around the fringes of forgotten Yewdale with the popular Tarn Hows. Rising from Coniston, peaceful woods are interspersed with openness and tremendous views, particularly when looking back over Coniston Water or to the mountains of Coniston Old Man and Wetherlam. The waters of Tarn Hows represent the physical high point and cannot fail to seduce, before descent by Tom Gill leads to one of the most classic Lakeland farms: High Yewdale Farm, with its famous spinning gallery. A round of Yewdale follows, with the row of yew trees in front of High Yewdale Farm indicating the return via Black Guards to Coniston. While there is quite a bit of ascent and descent, the going could never be described as laborious. Coniston Water is some 5 miles (8km) long and reaches a maximum depth of 184ft (56m). It is the third largest of the Lakeland lakes and was once an important fish source for the monks of Furness Abbey. Many of their iron bloomery and charcoal burning sites remain intact around the lake shore. The copper mines were revitalised around 1859, and some 800 men worked in Coppermines Valley above the village. The railway was axed in the early 1960s and the village now relies principally on tourism.

Lake stories
Speed ace Donald Campbell was killed on Coniston Water in 1967, attempting to beat his own water speed record of nearly 300mph (480kph). His boat, *Bluebird*, became airborne and crashed, but in 2001 it was raised from the bed of the lake. His body was also later recovered and buried in the village cemetery. Coniston Water is also the heart of 'Swallows and Amazons' country. Author Arthur Ransome spent idyllic childhood holidays at Nibthwaite, at the southern end of the lake, visited many times throughout his life, and lived for a while on the eastern shore. The lake in the stories is a hybrid of Coniston and Windermere, but Yewdale and the fells above are unmistakably the setting for the fourth of the 'lake country' novels, *Pigeon Post*.

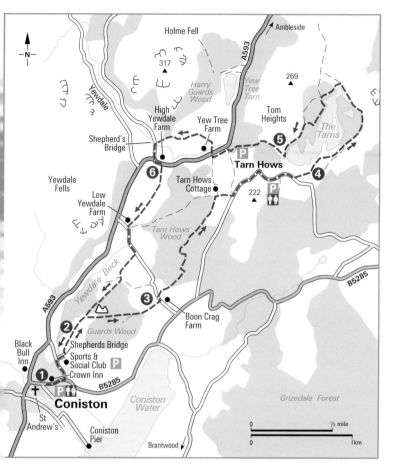

1. Exit the car park, cross Ruskin Avenue, and turn right on Tilberthwaite Avenue. In a few hundred paces, turn left on Shepherds Bridge Lane. Follow this beyond the Sports and Social Club to Shepherds Bridge, over Yewdale Beck. Cross and go immediately left. A short path leads to a kissing gate and enters a field. Bear diagonally right towards a rocky outcrop and oak trees, then continue to the right of a stone wall to a gate beside a renovated stone building (information panels inside).

2. Pass the building on the left. Ascend to pass through a gate. At a waymarked post fork right and rise diagonally right to a little gate through the stone wall, which encloses a plantation. Climb steeply to the top of the hill through the Scots pine. Pass through a gap in a wall and follow the obvious path descending through Guards Wood. Continue down a field track to a gate and stile onto a lane.

3. Go left, then in a hundred paces go right through a gate. Follow the grassy track winding up through fields. After a couple of gates it runs alongside the larch plantation of Tarn Hows Wood. Continue ahead to reach a surfaced track. Tarn Hows Cottage is below to the left. Go right up the track to a road and turn

left. Pass Tarn Hows car park then find a track bearing off left above the tarn. It's briefly indistinct across the grass but quickly becomes very clear again.

4. Follow the track to make an anticlockwise circuit of the tarn. Descending left at the first fingerpost offers a rougher and more interesting (and usually quieter) alternative for a while, but the main track is the easiest to follow. At the end is a little dam.

5. Turn right just before the dam and descend the rocky path to the right of the beck. At the bottom go left across the footbridge, then across the car parks to another footbridge and a gate. Follow the field-edge path to another gate opposite Yew Tree Farm. Cross the road and enter the farm access track, then bear right on a well-made track (a foot and cycle route). Follow this until a final gate leads onto a road. Turn left over Shepherd's Bridge and walk to the main Coniston road.

6. Cross and go left. Opposite High Yewdale Farm, a path leads right along a line of yew trees. At the end of the field bear right, across fields. At Low Yewdale farm go left of the barn, cross a bridge, and follow the track to a gate and Cumbria Way sign on the right. Cross the field. Beyond a wall the track ascends then bears right, alongside a plantation. Continue, to enter the trees, and follow the track through the wood. Descend to join the outward route at Point 2 and retrace your steps from there.

Where to eat and drink
There is plenty of choice in Coniston (see also Walk 25). The Black Bull Inn does good bar meals (huge portions!), and right next door is the award-winning Coniston Brewing Company, run by the son of the pub's owners, so there's always a fine choice of ales. There is also a good café, Herdwicks Café, at Yew Tree Farm.

What to see
The Victorian philosopher and art critic John Ruskin lived at Brantwood, across the lake, from 1871 until 1901. He was buried at St Andrew's Church in Coniston. His grave is marked with a large cross carved from local green slate. Designed by his secretary, Lakeland authority W G Collingwood, it depicts aspects of Ruskin's work and life.

While you're there
The restored steam yacht *Gondola*, built in 1859, was relaunched on 25 March 1980. Now operated by the National Trust, it plies Coniston Water every summer. The trip starts at Coniston Pier, passing Coniston Hall and stopping at Brantwood before returning.

A CLIMB ON SWIRL HOW

DISTANCE/TIME	8 miles (12.9km) / 5hrs
ASCENT/GRADIENT	2,820ft (860m) / ▲ ▲ ▲
PATHS	Well-defined mountain paths and tracks
LANDSCAPE	High mountain
SUGGESTED MAP	OS Explorer OL6 The English Lakes (SW)
START/FINISH	Grid reference: SD303975
DOG FRIENDLINESS	Off lead on mountain ridges, but sheep graze Prison Band in summer
PARKING	Coniston car park by tourist information centre, or at Sports and Social Club on Shepherds Bridge Lane
PUBLIC TOILETS	At car park
NOTES	Walk not advised in poor visibility

Popular with tourists, Coniston Old Man is always busy at weekends and in summer. For an equally fine fell climb, you can try Swirl How instead, barely lower than the Old Man itself. Coniston is the best place to start, with crags already looming close at hand. Once you're through the green fields and woods surrounding the village, the walk deposits you in a huge stadium of broken stone, where grassed-over spoil heaps, mill races and mysterious flooded mine shafts all lie in the shadow of quarry-terraced mountainsides. Copper mining here probably dates back to Roman times, if not earlier. When some German miners, brought over in Elizabethan times to kickstart 'modern mineral mining' in Britain, started work, they were shocked to find the mountains already riddled with workings, which they referred to as 'the old men workings', suggesting one possible derivation of the name Coniston Old Man. Mining reached its peak in the mid-19th century, but ended in 1914. The hard Borrowdale volcanic rock made drilling difficult and slow, and some of the veins were over 1,000ft (305m) below ground and over 500ft (152m) below sea level. The ore was known as chalcopyrite (sulphide of copper and iron), which has a yellow-gold colour, not unlike fool's gold.

The high mountain

Today the deep shafts are flooded, and even innocent-looking levels pose hidden dangers. Rock debris often covers the old wooden platforms, making it difficult to tell whether you're standing on solid rock or trusting your fate to rotten timber. Beyond the mines you pass Levers Water, a natural tarn dammed by the miners for a supply reservoir. The excitement begins at the pass of Swirl Hawse. From here, climbing Prison Band takes you into rocky terrain – steep, but hardly ever serious enough for the use of hands. Soon you're at the huge summit cairn looking across the grassy whaleback of Brim Fell to the Old Man. The connecting route from here is relatively easy. Purists and connoisseurs, however, will continue on, taking the little path that rakes across the high sides of Brim Fell to Goat's Hawse, a boulder pass between Dow Crag and the Old Man. The best view of Dow's magnificent climbers' cliffs and buttresses is from the shore of Goat's Water. And what more fitting way to end the walk than on Walna Scar Road, where the Romans transported their copper ore, over the mountains to the port of Ravenglass.

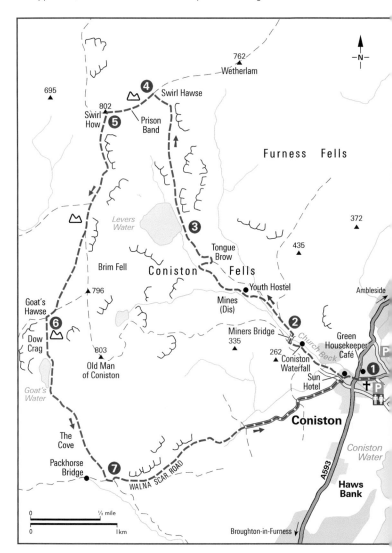

1. Turn left out of the main car park in Coniston to pass St Andrew's Church, then keep left to cross Church Bridge. Turn right immediately up a narrow lane. After passing the Sun Hotel go right on a track signed 'Levers Water, Coniston Old Man'. At Dixon Ground Farm bear left and continue parallel to Church Beck. Ascend to the old Miners Bridge above waterfalls.

2. Cross the bridge and turn left alongside the beck to the vast area of the Coniston copper mines. Take the left fork, pass beneath terraced cottages and walk past the youth hostel. After a steep section, turn right, signed 'Levers Water', near a water treatment works. At the next junction, above heaps of quarry spoil, follow the track doubling back right. It twists once more then climbs steadily up the slopes of Tongue Brow to Levers Water.

3. Keep right of the tarn along a path into the side valley of Swirl Hawse Beck, climbing steadily up to the high pass of Swirl Hawse, between Swirl How and Wetherlam.

4. On reaching the pass, turn left and climb up a rough path that scrambles over the rocks of Prison Band to reach the cairn on Swirl How's summit.

5. Turn left along the cairned ridge path, descending to a saddle between Swirl How and the grassy whaleback of Brim Fell. As you start to climb again, watch for a narrow path branching off to the right; this rounds the high sides of Brim Fell for a direct route to Goat's Hawse, the pass overlooking Goat's Water.

6. On reaching the pass, descend towards Goat's Water. A rough and rocky route traces the eastern shores of the tarn, overlooked by the cliffs of Dow Crag, before swinging left into the grassy bowl known as The Cove.

7. The path meets the Walna Scar Road, actually a stony track. Turn left to follow the ancient road round the south side of the Old Man. Lower down, the road becomes a tarmac, hedge-lined lane. Pass Old Furness Road, then take the lane on the left, rejoining the outward route by the Sun Hotel.

Where to eat and drink
In the centre of Coniston there are several pubs and cafés (see also Walk 24). The Sun Hotel is a 16th-century inn set just above the village, passed on both outward and return routes. Easier to overlook, the Green Housekeeper café on Yewdale Road is a very friendly place with a wide-ranging and eclectic menu.

What to see
The miners and quarrymen certainly left their mark on the Coniston fells, but they were sculpted on a far grander scale by Ice Age glaciers. One tell-tale imprint left behind from the Ice Age can be seen in front of you as you cross Miners Bridge: low, smooth slabs of rock scored by long scratches or shallow grooves. Known as striations, these marks were made by stones embedded in the ice.

While you're there
Visit the Ruskin Museum in Coniston, set up by John Ruskin's secretary W G Collingwood, both as a memorial to him and as a guide to the area's heritage. There are exhibits on the geology of Coniston and its copper mines. The museum also has an extensive collection of Campbell family memorabilia, including photographs and press cuttings about Donald Campbell's fateful attempt at the water speed record on Coniston Water in 1967.

26 ACROSS BIRKRIGG COMMON TO BARDSEA

DISTANCE/TIME	8.4 miles (13.5km) / 3hrs
ASCENT/GRADIENT	845ft (258m) / ▲ ▲
PATHS	Paths and tracks, some field paths may be muddy, many stiles
LANDSCAPE	Low-lying, rolling limestone country, with coastal margin, woodland, open common and enclosed pastures
SUGGESTED MAP	OS Explorer OL6 & OL7 The English Lakes (SW) and (SE)
START/FINISH	Grid reference: SD301742
DOG FRIENDLINESS	Under close control on roads and where there's livestock grazing
PARKING	Any of the small car parks alongside the coast road just south of Bardsea
PUBLIC TOILETS	At start (community operated, donations invited)

Birkrigg Common is a wonderful open expanse of bracken, grass and low limestone scars, rising between the shores of Morecambe Bay and the gentle valley containing Urswick Tarn. Although only a lowly height, it offers splendid views encompassing the whole of Morecambe Bay and most of the Furness peninsula, with Black Combe and the Coniston fells prominently in view. Other Lakeland fell groups, the Yorkshire Dales and Bowland feature more distantly. A network of paths and tracks allow an intimate exploration of the countryside, which turns out to be remarkably varied and interesting.

Geology
The bedrock of Birkrigg Common is Carboniferous limestone. It outcrops only on the margins of the Lake District, most notably around Morecambe Bay and Kendal, but also around Shap and above Pooley Bridge. It was laid down in a shallow sea and once covered the whole of the Lake District, before the area was pushed up into a vast dome by earth movements. Subsequent erosion largely removed the limestone layer, exposing the volcanic core of the Lake District and leaving only a few outcrops of limestone around the fringes. Birkrigg Common is dry, as most limestone areas are. In the low-lying valley at Urswick, however, water has pooled to form the lovely little reed-fringed Urswick Tarn, which is a haven for waterfowl. Some groundwater contained in the limestone layer reaches the surface as freshwater springs out on the sands of Morecambe Bay.

Ancient settlements
The area around Birkrigg Common was always fairly dry and fertile, compared to the higher Lakeland fells, so it attracted the attention of early settlers. Little remains to be seen, though there is a small early Bronze-Age stone circle of

limestone boulders on the seaward slopes. A standing stone at Great Urswick, known as the Priapus Stone and thought to be associated with fertility rites, lies at the base of a roadside wall. Several tumuli are dotted around the countryside and a rumpled series of low, grassy earthworks represent the remains of an ancient homestead site. Above Great Urswick, a low hill encircled by a limestone scar bears a hill-fort – probably dating from the Iron Age, in the centuries preceding the Roman conquest. It's interesting to wander around and let your imagination run free at the ancient settlement sites. Very little is known about them, but there has been a continual human presence in the area for over 4,000 years.

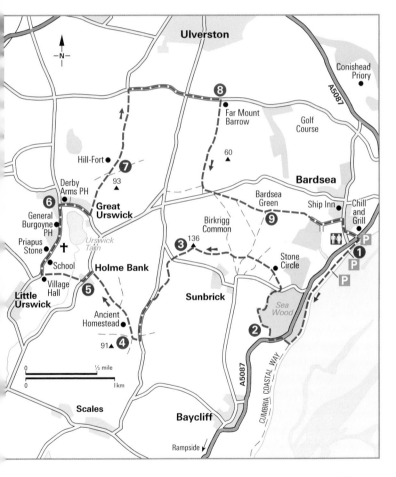

1. Follow the shore along to Sea Wood. At the far end of the wood turn right and ascend near its edge to the road. Turn left up the road to a small layby, then right at a gate just above into upper Sea Wood.

2. Follow a path around the top edge of the wood, keeping left at any forks, then descend to leave the wood at a gate. Cross a road and follow a grassy path through bracken on Birkrigg Common. Fork left to a wall corner then

keep left to a stone circle. Follow any grassy path to the high skyline; the trig point at 446ft (136m) affords fine views.

3. Pass a bench then bear right to meet a road. Cross and walk past a wall corner, then parallel to another road as the common tapers to a cattle grid. Continue along the road, then turn sharp right along a walled track.

4. Cross a stile at the end of the track and turn right. Pass the site of an ancient homestead, then keep left of a wall. Cross a stile at a gate, then bear left to find a path down a valley to a gate. Turn right before the gate and follow a hedgerow across a slope to a house. Pass through the garden to a road, then turn left to pass farm buildings at Holme Bank.

5. Turn right, following signpost to 'Public Footpath Church Road'. Cross a ladder stile and footbridge, then bear slightly left to a village hall and road. Cross the road and turn right to pass a school. Just after the entrance, the Priapus Stone is incorporated into a wall on the left. Pass the parish church in Great Urswick.

6. Turn right at the Derby Arms pub. At the crest of a slight rise, turn left up a steep track signed 'Footpath Red Lane'. Follow the track until there's a gate across it. Bear left through a second gate and walk straight ahead, keeping right of a limestone edge, the site of an ancient fort.

7. Where the limestone edge ends, follow a wall down to another gate, then go straight on. Cross a stile on the right and, on the other side of a gateway, cross a stile on the left. Walk straight on and enter a short track to reach a road junction. Turn right, continue across a crossroads, and on to the next farm.

8. Turn right before the first house of the farm complex along a bridleway sign-posted 'Bardsea Green'. Cross a stile by a gate and keep left to meet a road on Birkrigg Common. At a three-way signpost, follow the obvious path signed for Bardsea Green, initially parallel to the road, then parallel to a wall.

9. Keep left at a fork, then go through a gate and follow a track downhill to join a road. Keep left at a junction, up into Bardsea, then right at a T-junction, following the road down to the shore and back to the start.

Where to eat and drink

In Great Urswick, the General Burgoyne has a good reputation for food and drink and the Derby Arms is a great place for a refreshing pint, but neither is open every lunchtime. In Bardsea the Ship Inn, open from noon daily, offers real ale and good food. The Chill and Grill, right by the start, is seasonal and has outdoor seating only.

What to see

Sea Wood belonged to Lady Jane Grey, Queen of England for only nine days in 1554. It is managed by the Woodland Trust. Information boards at the access points list the tree species, flora and fauna you'll find here.

While you're there

Explore nearby Ulverston, with its cobbled Market Street. Ulverston is the birthplace of Stan Laurel and home to a Laurel and Hardy museum. Conishead Priory, between Ulverston and Bardsea, is a Buddhist study centre with a pleasant woodland trail.

27

EXPLORING THE GREAT LANGDALE VALLEY

DISTANCE/TIME	2.5 miles (4km) / 1hr 15min
ASCENT/GRADIENT	190ft (58m) / ▲ ▲
PATHS	Stony tracks (some enclosed) and rocky paths
LANDSCAPE	Meadows and fell in valley bottom
SUGGESTED MAP	OS Explorer OL6 & OL7 The English Lakes (SW) and (SE)
START/FINISH	Grid reference: NY295063
DOG FRIENDLINESS	Some fields grazed by sheep, so take care towards Oak Howe
PARKING	Choice of National Trust (Stickle Ghyll) or National Park Authority (New Dungeon Ghyll) pay-and-display car parks near the head of Great Langdale
PUBLIC TOILETS	National Trust Stickle Ghyll car park

Great Langdale – literally the big, long valley – has always played a key role in the story of the Lake District. In the 1920s there was a slightly unseemly row here, between outdoor enthusiasts and conservationists. The former, led by T E Leonard's Holiday Fellowship, wanted to build a campsite at the head of the dale in Mickleden, closer to the fine crags and mountains that inspired them. The latter, under the leadership of Dr G M Trevelyan opposed this intrusion into a landscape barely touched by human intervention for 200 years. The two men were pioneers of a new way of seeing the countryside, both passionately committed to its recreational value to the common man. After a few public letters, Leonard relented. The Holiday Fellowship built their encampment at Wall End Farm and Trevelyan bought up much of the upper valley and donated it to the National Trust. It was a measure of Langdale's hold on the popular imagination that things had come this far.

Perfect stone

Five thousand years ago the valley would have looked very different, without the farms and field boundaries established from medieval times. On the high slopes of the Langdale Pikes, the shapely crags that form the valley's northern boundary, neolithic man had discovered the perfect stone for shaping into axes. Imagine a world without metal, and then the impact a 'factory' that could turn out thousands of sharpened stone blades would have had. Axes made with Langdale's distinctive stone have been unearthed from neolithic sites all over Britain and Ireland and even a few in Europe. These were the tools that cut down the trees that allowed farmers to farm, and settlements to grow. Neverthless, it would be several thousand years after those first farmers cleared the upper reaches of this valley that there was anything obvious for us to see.

Stone walls

Walking through the valley now it is the stone walls that most obviously draw our attention. The valley floor is separated from the open fell by a 'ring garth'. Perhaps 13th century in origin, it would have protected the open valley fields from the beasts grazing on the upland 'waste'. Later field divisions followed, as agricultural techniques improved and the current field pattern would have been established pretty much as we see it today by the end of the 18th century.

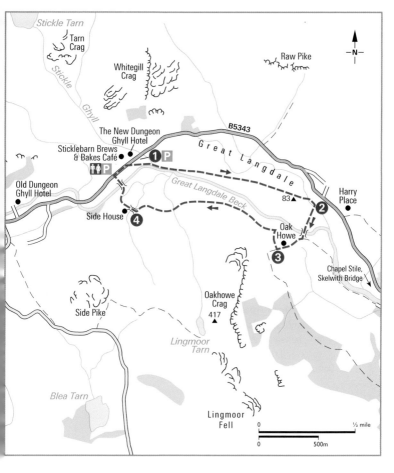

1. Locate a right of way at the back of the National Park Authority New Dungeon Ghyll car park. Follow this enclosed byway down the valley for nearly a mile (1.5km). After crossing a small beck turn right, signposted 'Chapel Stile and Ambleside'. In around 100yds (91m) turn right again at another fingerpost.

2. Follow the stony track across the virtually flat valley bottom. A gated bridge takes you over Great Langdale Beck and on the far side turn right up a farm track heading for a white farm building at Oak Howe.

3. Beyond the buildings turn right at a signpost on a footpath skirting the flank of the little hill and descending to a gate. Beyond this a stony track follows the base of the open fell with a wall on the right. The path ascends gradually and is rough underfoot in places. The ascent continues to a high point beyond a single slate bridge, with excellent views to Crinkle Crags and Bowfell at the valley head. The walls converge to a gate. Beyond this it descends briskly towards buildings at Side House.

4. Through a gate continue on a level path, cross a footbridge and pass through a kissing gate into the farmyard. Bear right along the access track to a bridge over Great Langdale Beck. Continue, emerging on the main valley road opposite the National Trust's Stickle Ghyll car park. Turn right if you left your vehicle in the National Park Authority car park.

Where to eat and drink

The Sticklebarn Brews & Bakes, a café at the top of the National Trust car park at the start, is the nearest and caters for most tastes. There's a huge open-air seating area out front, perfect for watching the sun go down over the surrounding fells. Near by the Old and New Dungeon Ghyll hotels also offer good food and beer.

What to see

You'll see a number of isolated ash and elm trees on this walk, their growth clearly stunted by pollarding at some time in the past. This wasn't done for ornament, but to create a reliable supply of foliage. Their leaves, along with those from holly, oak and willow trees, were fed to sheep, overwintering in the meadowlands of the valley bottom.

While you're there

Carry on up the minor road at the head of the valley and pass over the col towards Little Langdale (visited by Walk 23). Just beyond the col itself is Blea Tarn, beneath the slopes of Blake Rigg. A short stroll from the car park at its far end reveals one of the most photographed views in the Lake District.

28

ST JOHN'S IN THE VALE

DISTANCE/TIME	5 miles (8km) / 2hrs 45min
ASCENT/GRADIENT	1,115ft (340m) / ▲ ▲ ▲
PATHS	Grassy paths and track, 4 stiles
LANDSCAPE	Open fellside and river dale
SUGGESTED MAP	OS Explorer OL5 The English Lakes (NE)
START/FINISH	Grid reference: NY318195
DOG FRIENDLINESS	Under control at all times; open fellside grazed by sheep
PARKING	Car park at Legburthwaite, head of St John's in the Vale
PUBLIC TOILETS	At car park

With St John's in the Vale to the east and the Naddle Valley extension of Thirlmere Valley to the west, Naddle Fell forms an attractive little upland area that runs north from the end of the Thirlmere Reservoir towards the great northern fells of Blencathra and Skiddaw. Its three tops – Wren Crag, High Rigg and Naddle Fell itself – straddle a shoulder of craggy outcrops, sprinkled with a mix of bracken and ling heather. Tarnlets fill many of the hollows, rowan and Scots pine abound, and despite the presence of higher fells all around and roads in the dales below, this rugged fell has great charm and a surprising sense of isolation. This walk rises from Legburthwaite, at the head of the valley of St John's in the Vale, to traverse the length of the fell. Despite its higher neighbours it has a lovely, sunny disposition and is a pleasant place to linger on a warm summer's day. Sunsets seen from here over Castlerigg stone circle and Keswick can be spectacular. The walk along the top offers unparalleled views of the great bastion of Castle Rock, and north to Skiddaw and Blencathra, before dropping to the hidden little Church of St John's in the Vale. Finally it returns along the vale itself.

The Church of St John's in the Vale

As you enter through the little iron gate and archway of overhanging yew, the proportions of this slate-roofed, low, narrow stone building immediately seem just right. With the parish history related on its assembled headstones, it is a building in perfect harmony with its natural surroundings. The quiet road that runs past was once of greater importance, and linked communities on both sides of the high shoulder. Undoubtedly there has long been a church on this site, and although the present building dates from 1845, headstones outside predate this considerably. It is thought that a reference in the chartulary of Fountains Abbey to 'dommus sancti Johannis' – a house of St John – may refer to a church on this site in the 13th century. Otherwise the earliest definite reference to St John's is in 1554. The sundial is inscribed 'St John's Chapel, 1635', and a silver chalice (not kept within the church) was gifted in 1659.

The registers within the church date from 1776 onwards. The church was once part of the parish of Crosthwaite, which stretched from the top of the hill just outside Keswick to the top of Dunmail Raise, and included Thirlmere, Helvellyn and the stone circle at Castlerigg.

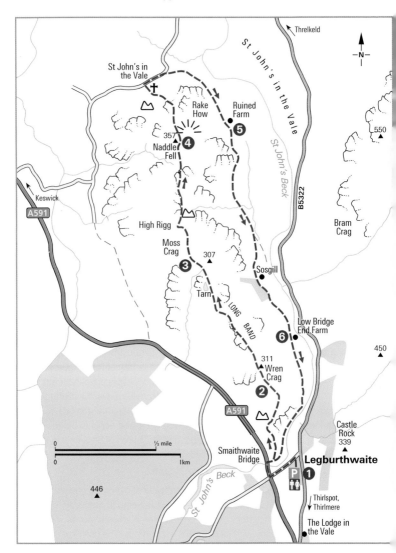

1. At the head of the car park a small gate leads onto the old road. Turn left down the lane to the verge of the busy A591. Turn right along this and cross Smaithwaite Bridge to a stile over the wall to the right. Cross it and take the path ahead, soon forking left and starting to climb. This leads through a stand of Scots pine with fine views to Castle Rock across the vale, then up to the open top of Wren Crag, where Skiddaw and Blencathra appear ahead.

2. Descend steeply into the dip and through the gap in the wall. Climb again to follow the crest of a line of rocky outcrops, Long Band. After a grassier stretch, bear left to a stile over a wire fence. Cross this then turn right along the fence to a little tarn in a hollow. Bear left, initially beside a ruined wall, and descend to reach a stile by a wall junction.

3. From the stile the path runs along the wall, climbing to pass through a corridor formed by the rocky knoll of Moss Crag. Beyond this, skirt left round a boggy area, then slant back right to the wall. When the wall turns sharp right, continue straight ahead and climb to the rocky summit of Naddle Fell, the highest point of this walk, which offers a superb view north to the high fells of Blencathra and Skiddaw.

4. Descend right from the cairn, then follow the wide path, which becomes very steep. Skirt left round buildings and turn right down the road. Just below St John's in the Vale church, a gate and bridleway sign lead to a recently 'improved' track. Skirt the foot of the fell along this track. Below Rake How pass a ruined farm surrounded by sycamores and a giant overhanging yew.

5. Keep along this track, passing through three gates and passing right of and above more ruins at Sosgill. A kissing gate leads into a mixed plantation. Continue along a narrower, rocky path and skirt just above Low Bridge End Farm (the tea room and garden are at the far end).

6. Continue along the path through a couple more gates until it meets the bank of St John's Beck, beneath Wren Crag. The path climbs, traversing a steep slope above the river, then swings right to a bracken-clad shoulder. Continue down to the stile that leads back onto the A591. Turn left and left again to return to the car park and the start of the walk at Legburthwaite.

Where to eat and drink
The King's Head lies to the south, at Thirlspot beside the A591, and offers bar meals and real ales. The Lodge in the Vale, closer to the car park, has a welcoming all-day coffee-shop. Low Bridge End Farm, passed near the end of the walk, has a tea garden serving home-made cakes and local ice cream in the summer months.

What to see
Guarding the entrance to St John's in the Vale, the great volcanic plug of Castle Rock forms a daunting and impressive landmark. Since the first ascent of its north face in 1939, the crag had become very popular for rock climbing. However, recent warnings of potential instability have kept many climbers away, though the sunnier South Crag remains popular.

While you're there
Threlkeld Quarry and Mining Museum, near Keswick, is one of the most fascinating attractions in the Lake District. Run by enthusiasts, it tells the story of mining in the Cumbria of old when coal, gypsum, graphite, lead, copper, zinc and many other minerals were extracted from the land. Located in an old quarry, it has a collection of locomotives and heavy machinery, a fine collection of mining artefacts and its own mine shaft.

LOW RIGG AND CASTLERIGG

DISTANCE/TIME	4.1 miles (6.6km) / 2hrs 30min
ASCENT/GRADIENT	623ft (190m) / ▲
PATHS	Grassy paths and tracks, a little road walking, 3 stiles
LANDSCAPE	Fell, fields and open valley
SUGGESTED MAP	OS Explorer OL4 The English Lakes (NW)
START/FINISH	Grid reference: NY306224
DOG FRIENDLINESS	Fields grazed by sheep so dogs should be under control throughout
PARKING	Responsibly around St John's in the Vale church and the Diocesan Youth Centre. Don't block the turning circle and note there is no onward road access beyond here, whatever satnav might say!
PUBLIC TOILETS	None on route

The stone circle at Castlerigg has been attracting tourists since the 17th century and featured in all the guidebooks that began to make the Lake District a destination from the 18th century onwards. There are 38 stones in a not-quite-round circle, and 10 more in a little grove to one side. Some have suggested there is a relationship between this apparently secondary arrangement and the tumulus on the summit of Great Mell Fell, several miles to the east. One can draw an alignment of a solstice sunrise, apparently, though this may be coincidental. What is known about the circle is scant. It dates from the late-neolithic/early Bronze Age, perhaps 3000–2500 BC and its one of a trio in the county that suggest there was a culture here of some sophistication. The other two – Long Meg and her Daughters near Langwathby and Swinside near Duddon Bridge – share Castlerigg's sense of majestic isolation, but beyond that there seems a great deal of conjecture. There hasn't even been a great deal of active archaeological investigation, though the National Trust did step in to 'rescue' Castlerigg as early as 1913 when there was a suggestion the stones could be fenced off and people charged for the privilege of walking among them. As recently as 2003 an axe, dated to around 3000 BC, from the Langdale 'factory', was recovered from a nearby field, so perhaps the people who produced this were associated in some to way to the monument builders.

Aged stones
No amount of speculation detracts from the grandeur of the place. The poet John Keats was clearly so impressed on his visit to the 'Druid Stones' in 1818 that it made up for a late dinner: 'We had to fag up the hill rather too close to dinner time, which was rendered void by the gratification of seeing those aged stones on a gentle rise in the midst of the mountains', he wrote to his brother the next day.

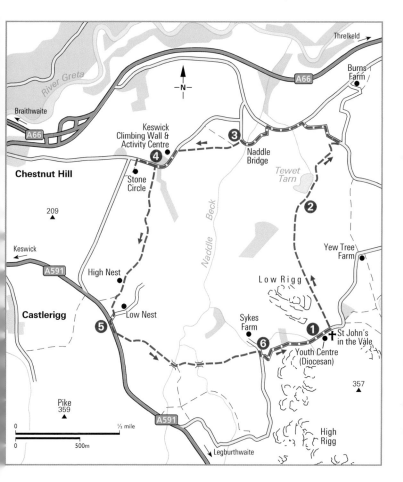

1. Opposite the church, climb a stile and follow the grassy path straight ahead. Keep right at a faint fork to climb a stile in a wall. The path continues through a grassy gap. Tewet Tarn comes into view ahead and the Castlerigg stone circle can be seen to the left beyond a white building in the distance. A broad grassy swathe leads down a gently sloping boggy area of open ground.

2. A gate leads you through a fence and, with Blencathra straight ahead, an obvious path continues to the right of the tarn and another gate. The path heads towards rock outcrops, where you turn right. Bear right beside a wall to pick up a faint track that swings downhill into a narrow enclosure. Drop to a gate in the bottom right-hand corner. Turn left along the road and left again at a T-junction. At the next junction, turn left with the signs to the stone circle and climbing wall. Just after Naddle Bridge, go through the farm gate on the left.

3. Always aiming for the white buildings of Goosewell Farm to the west, the right of way heads steadily uphill through a series of gates across the fields. Turn left along the road, passing the former farm buildings and climbing wall. As the road bends around to the right by a wood, look for a sign on the left to High Nest and the A591. Don't follow it now; you'll come back here shortly.

4. Continue along the road to the Castlerigg stone circle, accessed through a gate into the field on your left. Afterwards, return to the road and turn right, descending to the path sign passed earlier. Go through the gate and follow a faint path across three fields and to the right of a fenced woodland. When the trees end, continue beside the fence and then the wall to the farmhouse at High Nest. Follow the access road to a cattle grid. Here take the left turn signed towards the A591 and St John's in the Vale. Approaching the main road, you pass through a gate to a cattle grid on the access road to Low Nest. Turn right and emerge on the verge of the busy A591.

5. Turn left along the verge for a few paces to another footpath sign on the left. Go through the gate and descend the field towards an access road. Turn left along the road for a short distance then branch off right on a parallel path. Cross the road and keep ahead. Keep left, following the field boundary. At the bottom, go through the gate, carrying on along a muddy farm track for 120yds (110m) to a footpath sign just over a little bridge. Turn left across the field to a bridge over Naddle Beck. On the far side continue through a gate then across a field, heading for a kissing gate where a fence meets a short section of wall. Make your way up the craggy bank, bearing slightly left up the hill. Another kissing gate leads out onto a farm track.

6. Almost immediately, turn left up the Old Coach Road, following it all the way to the gate by the youth centre and the start.

Where to eat and drink

In summer it's worth seeking out the little Tea Garden at Low Bridge End Farm (at the Legburthwaite end of the Vale of St John). There are home-made cakes and local ice cream to go with the tea and coffee and the magnificent views of the surrounding fells. At other times, or if you need something more substantial, the Sally Inn and the Horse and Farrier are solid Jennings pubs in Threlkeld village, serving real ale and nice food.

What to see

The little Church of St John isn't in the Vale as you might suppose, but on a col between the Vale of St John and the Naddle Valley. Originally a chapel for the larger parish of Crosthwaite, it serves communities both sides of the ridge, once connected by the Old Coach Road, beloved by mountain bikers. Inside there's a memorial to Thomas Leathes Stanger Leathes, of Dalehead Hall, who opposed the Manchester Corporation's damming of Thirlmere until his death in 1877.

While you're there

Visit Threlkeld Quarry and Mining Museum, which tells the story of stone and mineral extraction in the area. There's an 'undergound' section ingeniously recreated beneath the vast former stone hoppers, a unique collection of excavators, steam-powered trains and plenty more to explore.

30

CALDBECK GREEN AND THE HOWK

DISTANCE/TIME	2 miles (3.2km) / 1hr
ASCENT/GRADIENT	230ft (70m) / ▲ ▲
PATHS	Grassy paths and tracks, 3 stiles
LANDSCAPE	Fields, riverside, limestone gorge and village green
SUGGESTED MAP	OS Explorer OL5 The English Lakes (NE)
START/FINISH	Grid reference: NY323398
DOG FRIENDLINESS	You are likely to encounter sheep throughout this walk so dogs should be on leads
PARKING	Caldbeck car park, close to village green on north side of village
PUBLIC TOILETS	On main street in Caldbeck village

'Howk' means scooping out in the old dialect of these northern fells, and it feels appropriate for this peculiar phenomenon, created by a change in the underlying rock. This is a limestone gorge with a waterfall, a Gordale in miniature. The Howk is surprising whichever way you approach it, but this walk brings you in from the top end. The Whelpo Beck looks benign until it slips away into woodland and suddenly disappears over an edge into a chasm; no wonder the old folk called it the Fairy Kettle. Beside it, the Fairy Kirk is a cave hollowed out of the limestone – a magical place deserving a supernatural name.

Auld Red Rover

Beyond, going downstream, is another immediate surprise. No sooner than you have stepped away from the little shelf-like viewing area of the Howk, you are confronted by another oddity. The high, stone-built mill that blocks your passage was once the home of Auld Red Rover, in its time one of the largest waterwheels in the country. Over 17 tons of metal held this monster together. It was over 42ft (12.8m) in diameter and at full pelt turned barely three times in a minute. Built in 1857, Red Rover powered a bobbin mill, the rest of which is remarkably well preserved beyond the wheel pit. Here is the coppice shed, where the dressed poles of wood were stacked to dry, and the turning floors where skilled men would craft millions of bobbins – reels and spindles – to serve the voracious cotton mills of Lancashire. Up to 60 men and boys worked here, the youngest lads perhaps only 10 years old when they were started on the basic tasks of peeling the bark off the hardwood logs. Cumbrian mills like this one supplied over half the bobbins to Lancashire's booming industry, and once there were over 70 of them, turning away. The last working mill was at Stott Park, near the bottom of Windermere. Here English Heritage allow you to see a working mill in action, with craftsmen showing how the bobbin makers spent their time.

Turned goods

The Howk mill was in production until 1924, by which time the biggest cotton mills were making their own bobbins, and new materials were starting to replace the traditional wood. The Howk produced hundreds of different items too, from 'dolly pegs', for washing clothes in your 'dolly tub' to tool handles. Potato mashers, egg cups, rolling pins, clog soles, even actual children's dollies all came out of the mill at one time or another, and the market for turned goods stretched beyond Manchester to Ireland and even Kolkata.

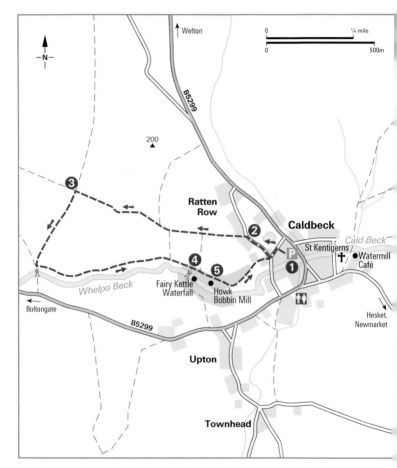

1. Leave the parking area at the far end of the car park, leading out onto the village green. Turn right and after 50yds (40m) turn right. As the road swings right, look for a bridleway sign on the left to Faulds Brow.

2. Follow this through a gate and up an enclosed track between hedgerows. Emerging into fields, ignore any turnings and keep straight ahead, with a fence on your right. After the next gate, turn right to a gate and stile. Beyond these, bear left across a faint field path towards a gate on the opposite side. Through this, turn left, heading for a gate at the top of the field. Bear half right up the

hill beyond this, picking out an ancient sunken lane at the brow, weaving between trees to a small gate. In a few more paces reach a stile on the left.

3. Cross this and walk across the bottom of a field to a kissing gate. Now descend with the wall, then a fence on your left. At the bottom, by the Whelpo Beck, turn left over a stone stile and follow the beckside path. The route narrows to step over a joining beck and pass through a kissing gate. A short flight of steps leads to another gate, where you bear right still heading downstream.

4. As the beck twists away into trees, the path rises up the bank to a gate in a hedgerow. Now a narrow, enclosed path descends towards the sound of rushing water. Pass a waterfall; the path then levels above a limestone gorge. A footbridge over the beck on the right affords a fine view of what is known as the Fairy Kettle. Don't cross the bridge, but continue to a flight of steep steps with more views into the gorge.

5. At the foot of the steps continue downstream, passing the ruins of the Howk bobbin mill. A level path leads back towards the village, swinging away from the beck and passing through a gated yard. Head half left (not sharp left) at the road and then turn right in a few paces to return to the car park.

Where to eat and drink
There are several options in Caldbeck, of which the pick is probably the Watermill Café at Priest's Mill. You'll find Fairtrade tea and coffee, home-made cakes, scones and gingerbread and more substantial menu items from sandwiches and ciabattas to Cumberland ham platters.

What to see
As you walk past the village green at the start of the walk, look for the duck pond down to your right. It's known as the 'Claydubs' and was once a clay pit, the clay used locally for making bricks and tiles.

While you're there
Explore the rest of Caldbeck village. Beyond the churchyard you'll find the pretty Priest's Mill, a restored cornmill, taking its power from the Cald Beck. By the church, St Kentigern's Well is supposed to be where the 6th-century saint once preached. And in the churchyard are the graves of John Peel, the legedary huntsman with his coat so grey (see Walk 34), and Mary Robinson, once far-famed as the 'Maid of Buttermere' (see Walk 43).

KESWICK'S WALLA CRAG ABOVE DERWENT WATER

DISTANCE/TIME	5.25 miles (8.4km) / 3hrs
ASCENT/GRADIENT	1,083ft (330m) / ▲ ▲ ▲
PATHS	Good paths and tracks, steep ascent and descent, 1 stile
LANDSCAPE	Woods, open fell and lakeside
SUGGESTED MAP	OS Explorer OL4 The English Lakes (NW)
START/FINISH	Grid reference: NY265229
DOG FRIENDLINESS	Fields and open fell grazed by sheep, open lakeside, suitable for dogs under control
PARKING	Lakeside pay-and-display car park, Keswick
PUBLIC TOILETS	In car park

At the foot of Borrowdale, often referred to as the most beautiful valley in England, the northern head of Derwent Water opens to Keswick and the northern fells with dramatic effect. While experiencing the considerable charm of the woods and lakeside, the highlight of this walk is the staggering view from the heights of Walla Crag. West across Derwent Water, beyond Cat Bells, Maiden Moor and the secretive Newland Valley, stand the striking northwestern fells of Causey Pike, Sail, Crag Hill and Grisedale Pike. To the southwest rise Glaramara and Great Gable, to the north Skiddaw and Blencathra. Undeniably this is one of the most evocative viewpoints within the whole of the Lake District National Park.

This walk touches the lake shore before traversing the oak woods of Cockshot and Castlehead, to rise to the craggy top of Castlehead. A fine viewpoint in its own right, it is guarded on three sides by steep ground. Springs Wood follows, before ascent can be made to the steep open shoulder leading to Walla Crag. The metal strips seen in the track once provided grip for the caterpillar tracks of tanks on training manoeuvres here during World War II. Descent through Great Wood follows and a delectable stroll home along the shore of this beautiful lake.

Derwent Water

The lake is 3 miles (4.8km) long and 72ft (22m) deep and is fed by the River Derwent. Seasonal salmon, brown trout, Arctic char, perch and the predatory pike swim beneath the surface. There are four islands on the lake, all owned by the National Trust. The largest and most northerly is Derwent Isle. Once owned by Fountains Abbey, it was bought by German miners from the Company of Mines Royal in 1569. The island and part of its grand 18th-century house are open to visitors on a handful of days during the year. St Herbert's Island was reputedly home to the Christian missionary of that name in the 10th century, and monks remained in residence after his departure. By the path, just above Derwent Bay, is an inscribed slate plaque in honour of Canon

H D Rawnsley, who did much to keep the lake as it remains today. He was vicar of Crosthwaite, the parish church of Keswick, and one of Lakeland's greatest conservationists. In 1895 he became a co-founder of the National Trust. He was a campaigner against rude postcards and also encouraged Beatrix Potter to publish her first book, *The Tale of Peter Rabbit*, in 1900.

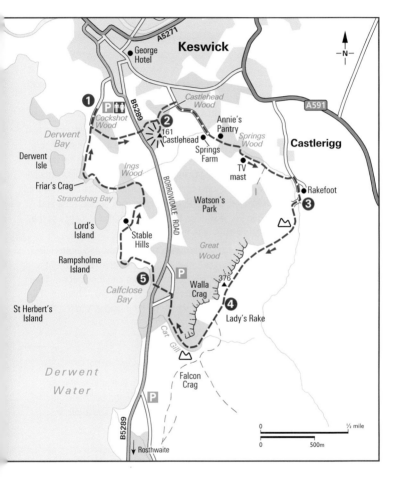

1. Proceed down the road to Derwent Bay. About 200yds (183m) after the entrance to the Theatre by the Lake, turn left along the track through Cockshot Wood. (This is the third path on the left.) Bear left at a fork. Exit the wood onto a fenced path between the fields and up some steps to the Borrowdale road. Cross the road and climb more steps to enter Castlehead Wood. Take the path to the left and then bear right to ascend the shoulder of Castlehead. Joining a path from the left, walk beside a fence. Then, at the fence corner, take the path on the right to climb steeply to the rocky summit of Castlehead and a fine viewpoint.

2. Descend by the same route to the fence corner and bear right. Ignoring a narrower path to the right, descend to a kissing gate leading on to an enclosed path. Follow this to Springs Road and turn right. When you reach Springs Farm, cross a bridge and take the track up through Springs Wood, passing to the right of Annie's Pantry. Bear right at the junction just before a bridge and follow the edge of the wood up past the TV mast. Ignore a turning on the right and continue to a footbridge left to join Castlerigg Road. Turn right along the road, keeping right at a fork, to reach another footbridge on the right.

3. Cross the footbridge and follow the path, ascending by the stone wall. Go through a gate, and walk out onto the open fell, ascending the steep grassy nose. Go through a kissing gate near a large cairn to gain access to a path that follows the edge of the crag. Take care: there is a steep unfenced drop. Those wishing to stay away from the cliff edge should continue to the left of the wall and take a higher stile. Follow the path, crossing the head of a gully, to climb onto the polished rock cap of Walla Crag, where the views are superb.

4. Continue along the main ridge path down to a stile over the wall. Cross and turn right. When faced with a choice, keep right, following the wall down to a gate. Beyond this, the descent into the gorge of Cat Gill steepens. One section on bare rock can be slippery. Entering Great Wood via a gate, continue steeply down. Bear right at a waymarked junction near a bridge over Cat Gill (towards Derwent Water). After a barrier, bear left. Cross a car park access lane and continue on, to locate a gap in the wall on the Borrowdale Road. Cross to the gap in the wall opposite and continue to the lake shore.

5. Bear right, following the shore path around Calfclose Bay. At Stable Hills you join a broad track. Follow this for 250yds (229m) and then bear left at a fork. After a bridge, keep to the path closest to the lake and it eventually leads to Friar's Crag. (Steps on the left lead out to the end of the small headland for a grand view down the lake.) Continue past the landing stages and the Theatre by the Lake to return to the car park.

Where to eat and drink

In Keswick you'll find the George Hotel, the town's oldest inn, which serves Jennings real ales, and has both restaurant and bar meal facilities. There is also a café overlooking Derwent Bay and another, called Annie's Pantry, en route in Springs Wood.

What to see

The rocky knoll of Friar's Crag, with its stand of Scots pines, is a famous lakeside viewpoint. At the foot of the crag, attached to rocks that are often submerged when the lake level is high, memorial plaques detail all the former mayors of Keswick.

While you're there

The Keswick Launch Company runs regular sailings around the lake. Landing stages en route include Ashness Gate, Lodore, High Brandlehow, Low Brandlehow, Hawes End and Nichol End.

HIGH ON CAT BELLS

DISTANCE/TIME	9 miles (14.5km) / 4hrs
ASCENT/GRADIENT	2,460ft (750m) / ▲ ▲ ▲
PATHS	Generally good paths, but slippery on bare rock on ascent of Cat Bells and indistinct above Tongue Gill, 2 stiles
LANDSCAPE	Fell ridge tops, quarry workings, woodland, riverside path
SUGGESTED MAP	OS Explorer OL4 The English Lakes (NW)
START/FINISH	Grid reference: NY246211
DOG FRIENDLINESS	No particular problems, though sheep roam the tops
PARKING	Parking area between Hawes End and Skelgill
PUBLIC TOILETS	Public toilets in Grange

Both Borrowdale and the Newlands Valley, like many parts of Lakeland, have seen extensive periods of industry from an early age. This walk takes you over Maiden Moor, from where you can see scree issuing from the workings of an old mine in Newlands. This is Goldscope, a name that first appears in records during the reign of Elizabeth I, who imported German miners to work here in a serious attempt to exploit England's own resources to reduce dependency on imports. The name is a corruption of 'Gottesgab' or 'God's gift', so called because it was one of the most prosperous mines in Lakeland. Copper was mined here as early as the 13th century from a vein 9ft (2.7m) thick. The mine also produced large quantities of lead, a small amount of silver and a modicum of gold. Copper ore was taken by packhorse to the shores of Derwent Water by way of Little Town. It was then transported to a smelter on the banks of the River Greta, at Brigham. From here the copper went to the Receiving House (now the Moot Hall) in Keswick, to receive the Queen's Mark.

The Rigghead Quarries in Tongue Gill produced slate from levels cut deep into the fellside and a number of adits are still open, though they are dangerous and should not be explored. But the real secret of these fells is wad, more commonly known as graphite, or the lead in your pencil. Its discovery dates from the early 16th century, when trees uprooted in a storm revealed a black mineral on their roots. Shepherds soon realised that the substance was useful for marking sheep, and later for making metal castings and as a lubricant. Its other uses included a fixing agent for blue dyes, glazing pottery, a rust preventative and polishing iron. Pencils, for which graphite was ultimately used, appeared around 1660 as wooden sticks with a piece of graphite in the tip. Keswick became the world centre of the graphite and pencil industries, the first record of a pencil factory here appearing in 1832. The Cumberland Pencil Company was set up in nearby Braithwaite in 1868, and moved to Keswick 30 years later. The old factory is now the site of a pencil museum.

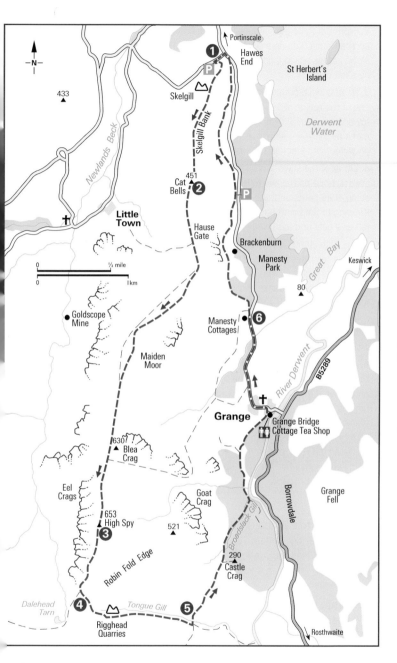

1. Take the path climbing from the eastern end of the car park. On a bend to the right, bear right at a fork in the path. This becomes stepped and rocky as it rises steeply. Continue uphill, clambering up small rocky outcrops before reaching Skelgill Bank. The onward route keeps to the centre of a grassy ridge, before rising through more rock outcrops to Cat Bells.

2. From Cat Bells descend easily to the broad col of Hause Gate. Go forward across Hause Gate on a clear path and onto the broad expanse of Maiden Moor, across which a good path leads to the summit of High Spy, marked by a tall cairn.

3. Head down a path towards the col housing Dalehead Tarn. Gradually, the top end of the ravine of Tongue Gill appears over to the left. Strike off southeast towards it about 500yds (457m) after leaving High Spy's summit cairn. Such paths as there are across to Tongue Gill are indistinct and invariably wet underfoot, but just keep heading for a fence.

4. Either of the stiles across the fence gives on to a path leading to a cairn at the start of a path down to Rigghead Quarries. Take care descending the steep slate paths until the gradient eases alongside Tongue Gill itself. Keeping to the south bank, follow the gill to a path T-junction, and there turn left to a gate and footbridge.

5. The path climbs gently and soon crosses a shallow col near Castle Crag. Go past the crag, descending, soon to enter woodland at a gate. When the path splits, bear right to cross a narrow footbridge spanning Broadslack Gill. Follow a path down to the banks of the River Derwent. Just before the river, cross a footbridge on the left and, a little further on, a second bridge. Keep to a path roughly parallel with the river until you reach a wall. Take a broad track following the wall and eventually walk out to a surfaced lane. Go right and walk up to Grange village, then left, following the road.

6. Just after Manesty Cottages, branch left onto a path climbing gently above the road to a gate. Through this, go forward onto a gently rising broad track and, when it forks, bear right, heading for a path above a wall. Pressing on beyond Brackenburn, the footpath, which affords lovely views of Derwent Water, soon dips to make a brief acquaintance with the road at a small quarry car park. Beyond this gap immediately return to a gently rising path – this is an old road, traversing the lower slopes of Cat Bells. Nearing Hawes End, keep right when the path splits. Turn left at the road and left again to return to the car park.

Where to eat and drink

Grange Bridge Cottage Tea Shop in the village of Grange offers a range of teas and snacks throughout the year (reduced opening hours in winter). Also within the village is the Grange Café serving refreshments.

What to see

Consider taking in the fabulous viewpoint at Castle Crag (the ascent and descent from the main path is clear enough, but it is steep and not suitable for very young children). To the east, the white-cottaged village of Rosthwaite sits comfortably against a backdrop of hummocky fells and steep crags, while northwards you'll see one of the finest views of Derwent Water, the Vale of Keswick and Skiddaw beyond.

BINSEY'S FARAWAY HEIGHTS

DISTANCE/TIME	2.5 miles (4km) / 2hrs
ASCENT/GRADIENT	722ft (220m) / ▲ ▲
PATHS	Road, moorland paths and tracks
LANDSCAPE	Upland farms and moorland
SUGGESTED MAP	OS Explorer OL4 The English Lakes (NW)
START/FINISH	Grid reference: NY235350
DOG FRIENDLINESS	Under control in sheep country, particularly at lambing
PARKING	At roadside pull-in on a minor road near to Binsey Lodge, off the Ireby to Castle Inn road
PUBLIC TOILETS	None on route

Binsey is not often on the itinerary of the casual visitor to the Lake District, and many of those you will meet as you complete this walk will be here for one reason alone – to tick off the summit in their relentless pursuit of the 214 fells Alfred Wainwright listed in his Pictorial Guides. The old man himself described it as an 'odd man out', 'a dunce set apart from the class', before going on to praise it as a gentle walk, with a very fine view. Pick a good day for this, perhaps when the northern Lakes are feeling a bit crowded, and you will be rewarded with exceptional vistas and not a little solitude.

Volcanic Binsey

The geology of Binsey is different from the Skiddaw massif that dominates its horizon to the south. Skiddaw, and the high, rolling fells that once made up its hunting forest, have a rock name to themselves. Skiddaw slate, a hard, metamorphosed sedimentary rock, is green in colour and can be seen in nearly every building in Keswick. Binsey's origins are volcanic, being largely made of basaltic andesite and rhyolite from a group of rocks known as the Eycott group. Eycott Hill is an undistinguished hill, squished between the limestone uplands of Greystoke and the great boundary fault at Mungrisdale. Blink at the Troutbeck turn on the A66 and you will have missed it to the north. According to computerised imagery, the view from the summit of Binsey on a clear day should extend to the tip of Slieve Donard, a mere 115 miles (185km) away across the Irish Sea, but this seems a little optimistic. What is more noticeable, this far north in Cumbria, is the proximity of Criffel, just over the Solway Firth. From this far northwestern summit, the top of Dumfries's favourite hill is closer to hand than the Pennines.

Devastating floods

Directly south, Bassenthwaite Lake curves gracefully up to Keswick, and Derwent Water beyond spreads before a fine background of high fells – Scafell Pike, the Langdales, Great Gable and Grisedale Pike can all be seen. To the west the Derwent Valley chugs gently down towards Cockermouth, Workington and the sea. This is a good spot to appreciate the vast extent of the River Derwent's catchment. On one fateful day in November 2009, over 12in (300mm) of rain fell on Seathwaite, at the head of Borrowdale, in 24 hours. Joined by waters from Thirlmere and the valley below you, it swept down the vale, meeting more torrents from Buttermere at one end of Cockermouth's Main Street. Tragically, one person died that day, but from these heights you'll be amazed that the floods didn't claim more victims.

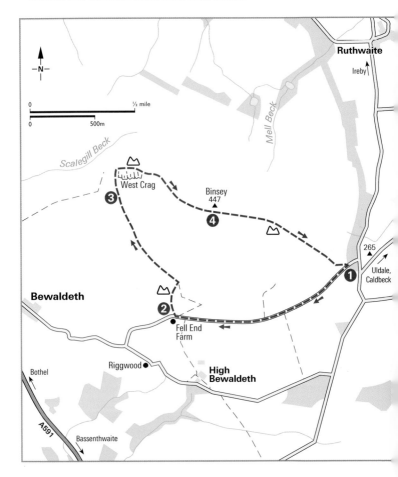

1. From the roadside parking area, walk down the quiet lane. There is very little traffic here and ample space at the side of the road to avoid it, but do keep an ear open for oncoming traffic.

2. In a mile (1.6km) or so you'll come to the farmyard at Fell End, where you should turn right, through a gate by a well. In the steep field beyond, stay with the left-hand boundary for a few hundred yards before striking off on a similar line towards a gate in the wall at the head of the field. You'll find it more convenient to pick the left-hand gate of the two you may be able to see. Through the gate, turn left, soon picking up a narrow trod contouring around

the fell, initially about 10 paces up from the wall, then maintaining its height as the wall slips away to the left. Continue on this line, indistinct in places but always traceable, eventually beginning to round the flank of the fell.

3. A lone hawthorn tree marks a path junction. Turn right here, heading up the fell. Bear left when the path splits. Step over a small beck to continue up into a boggy valley below the rocks of West Crag. The track becomes more substantial and is joined by another rising from the left. Continue upwards, the gradient now easing. Keep to the main path until you reach a short trail leading directly to the summit shelter. Take this.

4. From the rocky shelter, walk past the trig pillar and summit cairn, heading for the dark tarn of Overwater in the valley below. A wide grassy path soon begins to descend through the heather, finally bringing you down to a gate in the wall adjacent to the roadside parking area.

Where to eat and drink

The Snooty Fox at Uldale (northeast of Binsey on the Caldbeck road) serves good food and local beer. There's a fine beer garden round the back with views up to the fell. It isn't open at lunchtimes, however, and there's no food on Wednesdays. Well-behaved dogs and children are allowed.

What to see

Beyond the col, on the far (western) side of Binsey, you may be able to discern the distant lumps and bumps of a Roman fort. Now known by its British name, Caermote was probably not occupied for long, perhaps forming part of a defensive network during the building of Hadrian's Wall a dozen or so miles to the north.

While you're there

This is a quiet part of the National Park with a number of pretty settlements. Ireby, to the north of Binsey, clearly shows its origins as a medieval market town, with houses set around a square, though one suspects it was never terribly successful. Ireby's old church lies a mile (1.6km) or so out of the village, surrounded by fields. Built in the 13th century, it was replaced in the 1840s and is now cared for by the Churches Conservation Trust.

34 JOHN PEEL'S FELLS AT BASSENTHWAITE

DISTANCE/TIME	7.5 miles (12.1km) / 4hrs
ASCENT/GRADIENT	1,213ft (370m) / ▲ ▲ ▲
PATHS	Country lanes, bridle paths, footpaths (indistinct in places) and some rough walking through Burntod Gill
LANDSCAPE	Fells, fields and lakes
SUGGESTED MAP	OS Explorer OL4 The English Lakes (NW)
START/FINISH	Grid reference: NY230322
DOG FRIENDLINESS	Under control in sheep country, particularly at lambing
PARKING	Street parking in Bassenthwaite village
PUBLIC TOILETS	None on route

This part of the Lakes, at the 'Back o'Skiddaw' and across the fells of Uldale and neighbouring Caldbeck, is where John Peel and his pack of hounds galloped in pursuit of foxes. Although possibly the world's most famous huntsman, he was far removed from the stereotypical red-coated country gentleman. Peel was a tall, rough-spoken Cumbrian farmer with a loud voice. His coat of grey was made from everyday cloth. He wore knee britches, long stockings and shoes and a battered, well-worn beaver hat. To complete his outfit he carried a riding crop and a hunting horn. He liked nothing better than to spend a long day riding to hounds with his companions, returning home at dusk for a simple meal. Then they'd sit round the fire and indulge in an evening of heavy drinking before falling asleep in their chairs only to rise at dawn for another day on the fells.

John Peel was born at Caldbeck in 1776. At the age of 20 he fell in love with an Uldale girl called Mary White. They arranged to be married, but Mary's mother forbade the banns because 'They're far ower young'. Undeterred, Peel rode to Mary's house at midnight. She escaped from her bedroom window and they made for Gretna Green in Scotland, where they were married 'over the anvil' by the village blacksmith. Mary's mother accepted the situation and the marriage was ratified in the church at Caldbeck in December 1797. Mary inherited a property in Ruthwaite, where the family lived and farmed.

Peel died in 1854 and was buried in Caldbeck churchyard. That would have been the end of the story had not his friend John Woodcock Graves written a song about Peel. To the tune of 'Bonnie Annie', he dashed off 'D'ye Ken John Peel'. He joked, 'By jove Peel, you'll be sung when we're both run to earth'. Peel might still have been consigned to oblivion had not William Metcalfe, choir master at Carlisle Cathedral, composed and published a new tune for the song in 1868, which he was invited to sing at the annual dinner of the Cumberland Benevolent Institution in London.

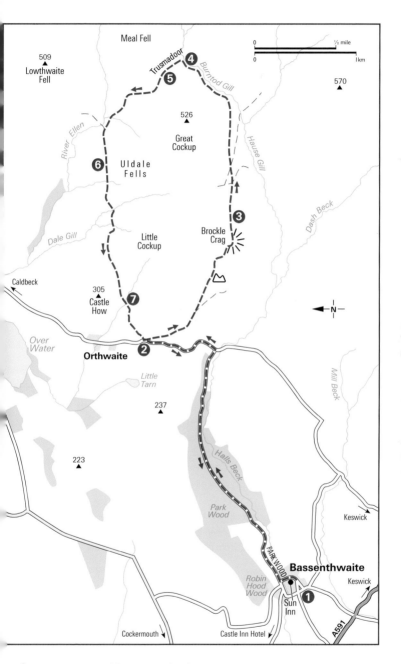

1. From the centre of Bassenthwaite village, pass the Sun Inn and turn right into Park Wood. Follow this for 1.25 miles (2km) to a T-junction, with a signpost pointing to Orthwaite, and turn left. Continue for about 650yds (594m) to a junction with a farm track coming in from the right, and a public bridleway sign.

2. Turn right along this track and through a gate signed 'Uldale Commons'. Follow the farm road to a public bridleway sign on the left. Take the bridleway and head uphill. It's a fairly steep climb to Brockle Crag before it levels out.

3. The bridleway heads downhill. Ignore another path to the right. Just before you reach a beck, strike off left (northeast) across pathless ground towards some tumbledown walls. From here, continue into the tight valley of Burntod Gill, joining a faint path along the way. This is loose and stony in places, crossing and recrossing the beck.

4. At the first notch in the hillside on the left, head up to the left away from the water through Trusmadoor, the pass between Great Cockup and Meal Fell. Keep straight ahead through the pass.

5. Bear left at an area of rushes just beyond a patch of slate. The path becomes less clear as it heads across two hillocks. When it fades to almost nothing over some boggy ground, keep heading northwest. You will then pick up a clearer path that swings left to round the shoulder of the fell.

6. Ahead of you on the horizon is Castle How with its halo of Scots pine. Where the clear path becomes less distinct, swing southwest to avoid losing too much height. You'll quickly pick it up again. Keep right immediately after a small ford, but keep left at subsequent forks.

7. Eventually you will see Bassenthwaite Lake ahead. When the path fades, follow the line of the wall on the right, returning to the farm track you followed earlier in the walk. Turn right here. Turn left at the road, then right at the junction, retracing your steps into Bassenthwaite village.

Where to eat and drink

Bassenthwaite is a small village with only one hostelry, but it's a good one. The Sun Inn has a reputation for serving excellent bar meals and a selection of real ales, both of which can be enjoyed in front of a log fire. If you fancy something a bit more formal, try the Castle Inn Hotel just outside the village.

What to see

Trusmadoor is a strange little pass, which Alfred Wainright described as 'the Piccadilly Circus of sheep in that locality'. Shepherds still use this route to move flocks from pastures on one side of Great Cockup to the other.

While you're there

Beside the A591 are the grounds of 17th-century Mirehouse, which lead down to the shores of Bassenthwaite Lake. Attractions there include adventure playgrounds and a nearby tea room set in the former sawmill. The house, still owned by the Spedding family who inherited it in 1802, contains fine collections of furniture, literary portraits and manuscripts reflecting the family's friendships with the poet Alfred, Lord Tennyson, artist Francis Bacon, and historian and essayist Thomas Carlyle.

WHINLATTER
FOREST PARK

DISTANCE/TIME	5 miles (8km) / 3hrs
ASCENT/GRADIENT	1,365ft (416m) / ▲ ▲
PATHS	Good forest paths and tracks, some rough walking, 2 stiles
LANDSCAPE	Forest, fells and lakes
SUGGESTED MAP	OS Explorer OL4 The English Lakes (NW)
START/FINISH	Grid reference: NY208245
DOG FRIENDLINESS	Off lead in forest provided they're under control; on lead on open fell
PARKING	Pay-and-display parking at the Visitor Centre
PUBLIC TOILETS	At Visitor Centre

Whinlatter Forest is a mixed plantation of trees ranging from Sitka and Norway spruce to Scots pine, Douglas fir and Lawson cypress. Look out also for native broadleaves such as birch and oak and the more exotic western hemlock and Japanese larch. Cumbria's conifer plantations were planted during the early part of the 20th century. Woodland resources were severely depleted by the end of World War I, particularly by trench warfare, so there was a need to rebuild and maintain a strategic timber reserve. The Forestry Act came into force in September 1919 and the new Forestry Commission's first planting in the Lake District was at Hospital Plantation, Whinlatter, in the same year. The forest provides a habitat for a wide range of wildlife and on this walk you may see roe deer, red squirrels, frogs, toads and foxes, and buzzards, peregrines and many other birds overhead.

One rare species you have a good chance of seeing, depending on the time of the year, is the osprey. A breeding pair of ospreys has been nesting close to Bassenthwaite Lake since 2001, the species previously having been persecuted to extinction in England more than 150 years ago. The huge nest, built by the Forestry Commission and the Lake District National Park Authority, is located in the forest above the lake and is subject to a round-the-clock guard once the female lays her eggs. Ospreys have a wingspan of nearly 5ft (1.5m) and are rich brown in colour with a white head and underside. They're fish eaters and you are most likely to see one hovering over the lake, its sharp eyes scanning the water for a fish before transforming itself into a feathered missile streaking down unerringly to snag its prey. Ospreys winter in Africa, but return to the Lake District in the spring to breed.

The lower viewing point in Dodd Wood is staffed from April through to the end of August, from 10am to 5pm. High-powered telescopes and binoculars are available during the breeding period. Cameras are also trained on the nest so that visitors can view live footage of the birds on a giant video screen at the Whinlatter Visitor Centre.

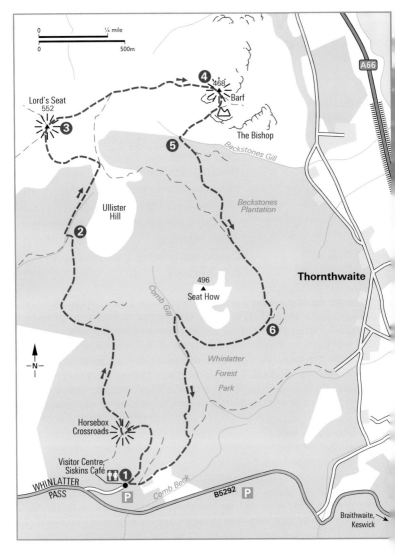

1. The walk starts by heading through the covered walkway between the Forestry Commission shop on your right and the public toilets on your left. Then turn left, following red, blue and green waymarks up the hill and past an adventure play area. On reaching a viewpoint, bear left after the benches, following the green markers to a T-junction. Turn left again to reach Horsebox Crossroads and the No. 2 marker post. Turn sharp right here and continue along the forest road, ignoring a track turning on the right near to marker post No. 3.

2. As the road makes a sweeping bend to the left, turn right onto a path marked by post No. 24. Head uphill through the forest onto the fellside to another T-junction. Turn left and keep on the path as it climbs and crosses a stile to reach the summit of Lord's Seat. On a clear day you should be able to

124

see the hills of southern Scotland as well as the high Lakeland fells to the south and east.

3. Leave the summit by following either of the paths on the east side of Lord's Seat. After crossing a peaty, often damp area, a single, drier path climbs to the summit of Barf. Below you and stretching away to the right is the Vale of Keswick with Derwent Water, dotted with islands, beyond. There's also a grand view over Bassenthwaite Lake.

4. Heading right – down the steep, southern side of the fell – you quickly encounter two paths. Take either, although the one on the right is slightly less exposed. If you choose this one, you will need to turn right in a short while to hug the southern edge of the escarpment. Carefully cross Beckstones Gill and go over a stile into Beckstones Plantation.

5. Turn left down the track, passing marker post No. 21. Keep ahead on the clear path, climbing steadily to a T-junction at marker post No. 8. Turn left onto the forest road and follow it to another T-junction at marker post No. 9.

6. Turn right and continue for 440yds (402m) to reach marker post No. 10. Go left down the grassy path. As this bends left, turn left along a narrower path with a red-topped post beside it. This weaves its way down beside Comb Gill to another forest road. Turn right at this junction, still following the red trail. Keep right when the track forks and right again at the next junction, at marker post No. 14. Follow this through a wooden barrier. The Visitor Centre is up to the right, or keep straight ahead for the car park.

Where to eat and drink

You could do a lot worse than dine at the Visitor Centre's Siskins Café. It's warm and friendly and has a good selection of food, with tasty hot soup being a favourite on cold days. If you're looking for something more substantial, drop down the Whinlatter Pass to Middle Ruddings Country Inn in Braithwaite, serving home-cooked food and real ales.

What to see

Walking through Beckstones Plantation, look for the white-painted rock on Barf's lower slopes – the Bishop of Barf. Legend states that in 1783 the Bishop of Derry had a wager with locals that he could ride over Barf to Whitehaven. The next day, he and his horse headed up the scree-covered fell. His wager – and his life – came to a sudden end when he slipped and plunged down the fellside. The rock marks the place where he fell.

While you're there

Don't miss Keswick Museum and its eclectic collection of exhibits, ranging from original manuscripts and memorabilia of the Lakeland poets, William Wordsworth and Robert Southey, to a bizarre 500-year-old cat. The museum is also home to the 'Geological Piano' set of musical stones, which once went to London and were used in a performance for Queen Victoria.

ANCIENT OAKS OF ARD CRAGS

DISTANCE/TIME	5.1 miles (8.2km) / 2hrs 45min
ASCENT/GRADIENT	1,606ft (490m) / ▲ ▲ ▲
PATHS	Road, narrow fell paths, some indistinct
LANDSCAPE	Heathery ridge flanked by steep slopes
SUGGESTED MAP	OS Explorer OL4 The English Lakes (NW)
START/FINISH	Grid reference: NY229201
DOG FRIENDLINESS	On lead on road and on fell
PARKING	Small car park in old roadside quarry at Rigg Beck
PUBLIC TOILETS	None on route

On this walk you can enjoy views of craggy fells and fine ridges. The landscape is very open, with gentle fields giving way to steeper slopes covered in bracken and heather. It's tempting to believe that the Lake District was always like this – bare, barren and wild. In fact, the natural state of the Lakeland fells, if humans had never set foot there or brought grazing livestock into the area, would be quite different. The climax vegetation would be deciduous forest, comprising oak and birch on most slopes, with alder in the boggy lowlands and rowan in the rocky clefts, leaving only the summits of the fells rising bare above the trees. If it's hard to imagine what this kind of forest cover would look like, then study the patchy oak woods on the steep southern slopes of Ard Crags and Causey Pike. Short, gnarled oaks in these locations are thought to represent the last remaining indigenous Lakeland forests. They are sessile oaks, meaning that the acorn cups sit on the twigs, rather than pedunculate oaks, where the acorn cups are on stalks (like the The National Trust logo).

Grazing sheep

Centuries of sheep grazing has led to the Lake District's current appearance; a process accelerated when distant monasteries encouraged large-scale grazing from the 12th century. Constant nibbling prevents woodland cover from regenerating, so that established trees simply get older and eventually die. The seeds can find no safe place to germinate unless protected from livestock and rabbits. Holly, hawthorn, gorse and bramble survive simply because they are so prickly, and many fine specimens of gorse can still be seen even on the sheep-grazed slopes on this walk. The open landscape allows walkers to enjoy the glorious views, the fell paths, unchoked by rampant vegetation and, in the case of Ard Crags, the purple flush of heather in high summer. Ard Crags, surrounded by plenty of loftier summits, isn't a particularly high fell, but you can see the highest Lakeland fells, including the Scafells, Helvellyn and Skiddaw, as well as groups of fells around Ennerdale, Buttermere, Wasdale and Langdale.

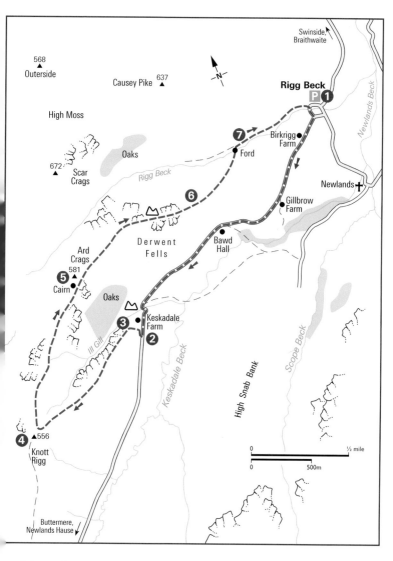

1. Leave the quarry car park at Rigg Beck and turn right along the road, rising gently past farms and fields. Pass Birkrigg Farm and Newlands Fell, Gillbrow Farm and Bawd Hall. The road descends gently across a more rugged fellside and reaches a sharply pronounced bend crossing the beck of Ill Gill. A steep slope covered in ancient sessile oaks rises to your right. Continue on the road for 350yds (320m) beyond Keskadale Farm.

2. Just after the fence up to the right ends, you'll see a tiny layby on the right. A faint trail heads sharp right from here – almost back on yourself – back towards the fence. You could now climb beside the fence to find the path on to the ridge, but it's easier to use the zig-zagging route that heads left from the fence corner before switching back to the right, after 100yds (91m), to return to the fence. Head uphill beside the fence for 250yds (229m), the sunken trail

obscured by bracken in the summer. You'll then see a gap in the bracken on the left. This marks the start of the path on to the ridge.

3. Don't be lured by a path to the left; stay parallel with a fence over to the right in the lower stages of the climb. The path is narrow as it ascends a steep slope, and there are some stony patches. Higher up the ground is boggy and the path is indistinct. After passing between two tiny fenced areas, it disappears completely. Look to the west now to spot a gentle, rounded summit and aim for it. This is Knott Rigg, 1,824ft (556m) high, surrounded by higher fells.

4. A clear path heads roughly northeast along the hummocky ridge. Mosses, sedges and rushes indicate wet ground. The path drops to a gap, then climbs uphill slightly to the right of the ridge. The ground cover is now heather, indicating drier ground. Gullies fall away to the right, then the summit cairn on Ard Crags is reached – at 1,906ft (581m), the high point of this walk.

5. Walking along the heathery ridge is like walking on top of the world, with a fine view over the Vale of Newlands. Bilberry and crowberry grow among the heather, providing an autumn feed for birds or passing walkers. The descent is in two stages, dropping first to a heathery bump, and then dropping more steeply past outcrops of rock.

6. Heather gives way to bracken as the gradient eases, then the path runs level onto a blunt, grassy ridge. Bear left at a fork in the path to descend to Rigg Beck stream and ford it. If a narrower crossing point is needed, look a short way upstream.

7. Climb up from Rigg Beck and join a clear path, turning right to follow it down the valley. The slopes are covered in bracken with occasional clumps of gorse. The path leads back to the car park.

Where to eat and drink
The nearest pub offering food and drink is the Swinside Inn, a prominent whitewashed building tucked against the forested little hill in the village of Swinside about 1.5 miles (2.5km) to the north.

What to see
Vegetation cover is in a slow but constant process of change. Bracken invades the rough pastures, but notice how it never grows on trodden paths or wet areas. Heather can tolerate wet ground to a certain extent, but not waterlogged ground, which is often colonised by mosses and tussocky moor grass. Even the bare rock is in fact covered with multicoloured blotches of lichen.

While you're there
Literary associations abound around Newlands. William Wordsworth penned some lines about Newlands Church; Hugh Walpole used the area as a setting in *The Herries Chronicle* (1930–33); Beatrix Potter's *The Tale of Mrs Tiggy-Winkle* (1905) mentions Little Town. Alfred Wainwright wrote that the valley 'hadn't changed in any way throughout 50 years of acquaintance'.

STONETHWAITE TO WATENDLATH

DISTANCE/TIME	5 miles (8km) / 3hrs 30min
ASCENT/GRADIENT	1,440ft (439m) / ▲ ▲ ▲
PATHS	Bridleways, fairly good paths and some rough walking, 3 stiles
LANDSCAPE	Fells, forest, tarns and lakes
SUGGESTED MAP	OS Explorer OL4 & OL6 The English Lakes (NW) and (SW)
START/FINISH	Grid reference: NY262137
DOG FRIENDLINESS	Sheep country so keep dogs under control
PARKING	By telephone box in Stonethwaite. Alternative parking (with public toilets) at National Trust car park in Rosthwaite
PUBLIC TOILETS	Watendlath and Rosthwaite

One stormy night in 1739, Francis 'Rogue' Herries brought his family to live in the house his grandfather built in Borrowdale. His son, David, 'woke again to see that all the horses were at a standstill and were gathered about a small stone bridge.' The 'hamlet clustered beyond the bridge' was probably Grange. From there they crossed over a hill to come at last 'into a little valley, as still as a man's hand and bleached under the moon, but guarded by a ring of mountains that seemed to David gigantic.' This is the village of Rosthwaite, and the Hazel Bank Hotel sits on the spot where the Herries house stood. However, this house never existed except in the imagination of the novelist Hugh Walpole (1884–1941) and between the covers of the four-volume series he wrote, collectively known as *The Herries Chronicles* (1930–33).

Walpole, one of the best-selling writers of his day, wrote over 50 novels. He bought a house above Derwent Water in 1923 and two years later announced that he was 'pinning all my hopes on two or three Lakes' novels, which will at least do something for this adorable place.' What he eventually produced over a five-year period was a romantic history of a Lake District family from 1730 to 1932. Woven into the Herries' story are the major historic events of the period. The Jacobite Rebellion of 1745 passes nearby in Carlisle, 'Rogue' Herries' son David dies at Uldale as the Bastille falls in 1789 and Judith, his daughter, gives birth to her son Adam in Paris as Napoleon is finally defeated in 1815. 'Rogue' Herries, soon notorious in Borrowdale for his wildness, completes his infamy by selling his mistress at a fair. His consuming, unrequited love for Mirabell Starr, a gypsy woman, drives him to wander the country for hundreds of miles in search of her. Finally at Rosthwaite, after 44 years in Borrowdale, he dies as Judith, the daughter of his old age, is born in 1774. Walpole's evocative descriptions enrich the enjoyment of walking through his stones and skies. They capture the essence of this wild and beautiful place.

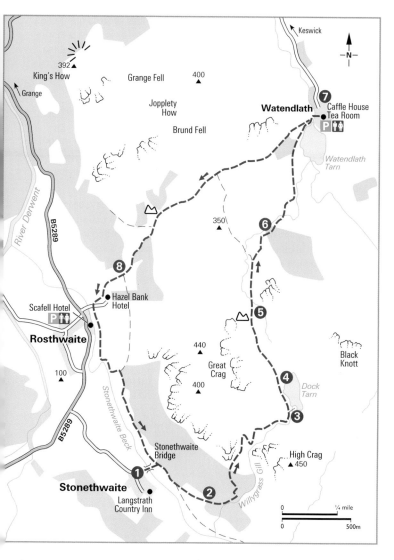

1. With your back to the parking area in Stonethwaite, turn right and walk down the track to Stonethwaite Bridge. Cross it, go through a gate and turn right onto the bridleway to Grasmere. Go through another gate and, after about 250yds (229m), look for a path off to the left, climbing to the left of a tiny sheepfold. This soon bends left to climb more steeply.

2. After crossing two stiles, continue steeply uphill on a paved path through oak woods. The path emerges from the trees still climbing. Cross a stile beside Willygrass Gill and follow the path to Dock Tarn.

3. Keep right at any forks to follow the path around the west side of the tarn. There are some rocky sections but the going isn't difficult. If the lower path is flooded, higher paths to your left lead in the same direction.

4. At the north end of the tarn the broad path continues above boggy ground in the direction of a gap between two low crags. A view opens up ahead with Ether Knott then the Skiddaw beyond. Be careful not to be lured off course by a faint trail to the right here; keep to the stony path. Just past a small rock pinnacle on the left, Watendlath comes into view and the path descends a rocky staircase to a kissing gate.

5. Go through the gate, cross the beck and follow the stone path across the bog. Turn right at a grassy junction and descend to a sheep pen.

6. Continue downhill to go through a kissing gate. Walk beside the stream, cross it and then follow the line of the wall to join a farm track. As a track comes down from the left, keep right to go through a gate and cross the old packhorse bridge into Watendlath.

7. From Watendlath recross the bridge, turn left and, at the fork, bear right to follow the bridleway sign to Rosthwaite. Walk uphill on this well-used route, go through a kissing gate and head downhill, passing a gate on the right and going through another gate, lower down. At the next gate a sign indicates that the path continues to Stonethwaite.

8. Ignore the sign and instead turn right through the gate in the wall. Cross the surfaced driveway of Hazel Bank Hotel and continue on the public bridleway to Stonethwaite. About 0.8 miles (1.3km) beyond the hotel, turn right at a fingerpost to return to the start of the walk.

Where to eat and drink

The Langstrath Country Inn at Stonethwaite is just the place for an end-of-walk meal, or you can relax with a pint and a bar meal in front of the log fire in the Scafell Hotel at Rosthwaite. You can also get a fine lunch in the Caffle House tea room at Watendlath, where, on a fine day, you can eat outside.

What to see

Just to the left of the pedestrian exit from the National Trust car park in Watendlath is a white farmhouse with a plaque on the wall proclaiming it to be the house of Walpole's fictional Judith Paris. Geese feed on the grass in front of the farm while ducks bob about in the water near the ancient packhorse bridge.

While you're there

The single track road to Watendlath from the Keswick–Borrowdale road is one of the most scenic in the Lake District. Half-way up you'll cross Ashness Bridge, with the much-pictured backdrop of distant lakes and mountains. Also worth seeing are the spectacular Lodore Falls, the subject of Robert Southey's poem 'The Cataract of Lodore' (1820). He wrote 'How does the water come down at Lodore?' Formed by the water rushing down the beck from Watendlath Tarn and tumbling over some large stones, the falls are just behind the Lodore Falls Hotel.

ALONG THE STYHEAD PASS FROM SEATHWAITE

DISTANCE/TIME	5.75 miles (9.2km) / 2hrs 30min
ASCENT/GRADIENT	1,673ft (510m) / ▲ ▲ ▲
PATHS	Stony paths and tracks; care needed on descent
LANDSCAPE	Rugged and mountainous, with two high tarns
SUGGESTED MAP	OS Explorer OL4 & OL6 The English Lakes (NW) and (SW)
START/FINISH	Grid reference: NY235122
DOG FRIENDLINESS	Good for fit, active dogs; under strict control near sheep
PARKING	By roadside below farm
PUBLIC TOILETS	At Seathwaite Farm

Seathwaite has long been a gateway to the high fells of Lakeland, including Glaramara, Great Gable, and the highest of them all, Scafell Pike. Routes from here also lead to the valleys of Wasdale and Great Langdale. This walk is a great introduction to the delights and fascination of the high fells. While it doesn't top any of the surrounding heights, it does rise to an altitude of some 2,050ft (625m) among some breathtaking mountain scenery, including the famous tarns of Styhead and Sprinkling. The walk is technically straightforward, but because of the altitude and the rapidly changing weather conditions you are likely to encounter in the Lakeland fells, everyone undertaking this round should be equipped for mountain walking.

Once an important packhorse route, this ancient highway, known as Styhead Pass, linked Borrowdale to Wasdale – from the heart of mountain Lakeland to the west coast. Along its length travelled illicit wad (a source of locally mined graphite) and whisky to be exchanged for brandy and spices at Whitehaven and Maryport. Sty Head is a famous mountain crossroads; as well as to Wasdale, routes from here lead up to Scafell Pike, Great Gable and Esk Hause. The rescue box contains a stretcher and first aid equipment. It has proved to be a lifesaver on more than one occasion. In extreme weather, those caught out in these hills have been known to crawl inside to seek shelter.

Sprinkling Tarn and Great End

Although Sprinkling Tarn is at an altitude of some 1,970ft (600m), during the summer months its dark surface is often ringed by brown trout jumping for flies. It lies directly below the cliffs of Great End. These have little attraction for rock-climbers but are a great lure for winter ice-climbing. The unmistakable Central Gully is a classic route, but when westerlies blow snow off the summit plateau, great accumulations of snow form at its head. As volumes increase the snow becomes unstable and avalanches sweep down the gully. Many an unwary mountaineer has been avalanched out of this gully. Incredibly, fatalities are rare and the victims usually escape with broken limbs or just cuts and bruises.

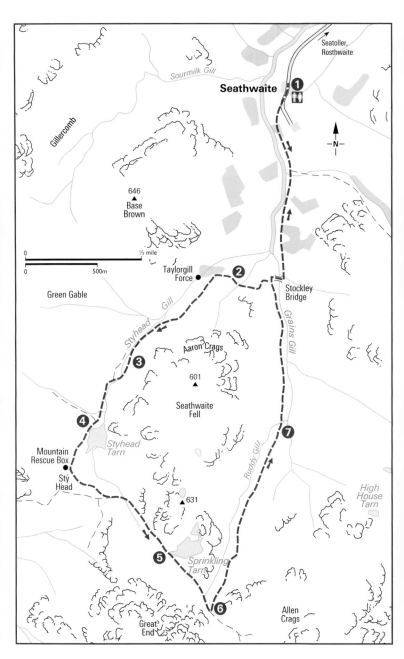

1. Pass through the cobbled farmyard and continue along the rough stony track up the valley. A few rises and dips among steep mounds (glacial moraines) lead to the ancient stone arch of Stockley Bridge, which spans Grains Gill. Cross the bridge, go through a gate and follow the track (in places reconstructed with pitched stone) up the hillside to a second gate.

2. Above the wall the way bears right, ascending to skirt the edge of the woods above the ravine of Taylorgill Force. A fence protects the edge and, although the great waterfall is hidden below, it is usually possible to hear its roar. Beyond this point the track follows a line just above the beck to reveal a series of little tumbling falls, rock slides and pools. Gradually the gradient eases off.

3. Beyond an area of rough stones and boulders, a small wooden footbridge crosses the beck. Take the bridge and continue a few hundred paces to Styhead Tarn. If conditions are favourable this is a good place to take a break and eat your sandwiches.

4. Traverse above the shore of the tarn then ascend to the mountain rescue box at the rough rocky col of Sty Head. Turn left (east) and follow the stony path uphill, keeping left at a fork in the route. Stay with the main track, ascending to reach the edge of the teardrop known as Sprinkling Tarn.

5. Keep along the track to pass beneath the dark and foreboding cliffs of Great End. At the halfway point beneath this, you meet the stream of Ruddy Gill tumbling towards you and then swinging off north (to your left). Above this point a great gully, Central Gully, cuts directly up the cliff.

6. Continue a few paces then drop down to cross the stream at large stepping stones. (In the – very rare – event that these are covered by flood water, it is strongly recommended to return the way you came, via Sty Head). Having crossed the stream, follow the path down the true right bank of Ruddy Gill (leading to Grains Gill). Once very badly eroded, this path has now been rebuilt using pitched blocks of rock. Although the descent is steep, and rather hard on the knees, the path is clearly defined: a tremendous achievement by the path-builders. However, there are still a couple of places where it narrows above a steep drop, so take care.

7. Continue more easily until a small footbridge leads across Grains Gill. The path leads eventually down to the gate above Stockley Bridge. Cross again here and head back to Seathwaite Farm.

Where to eat and drink

The nearest year-round sources of refreshment are the two pubs in Rosthwaite. Next door to each other, the Royal Oak and the Scafell Hotel both serve real ale and a range of bar meals.

What to see

Small, dark-red garnets can be found in the rocks of Grains, on the flanks of Seathwaite Fell above Grains Gill. These semi-precious gemstones are geologically interesting, though their small size (up to 5mm diameter) makes them worthless in monetary terms.

While you're there

Above the parking areas, well to the right of the tumbling waterfalls of Sour Milk Gill, are the waste tips of the disused wad mines. Seathwaite wad was once the richest source of graphite – pure carbon – in Europe, and these mines were so important that they were protected by armed guards.

SEATHWAITE AND THE DUDDON VALLEY

DISTANCE/TIME	5 miles (8km) / 3hrs
ASCENT/GRADIENT	850ft (259m) / ▲ ▲
PATHS	Paths, tracks, can be muddy below Seathwaite Tarn, rocky in Wallowbarrow Gorge, several stiles
LANDSCAPE	Craggy mountainside and wooded gorge
SUGGESTED MAP	OS Explorer OL4 & OL6 The English Lakes (NW) and (SW)
START/FINISH	Grid reference: SD229961
DOG FRIENDLINESS	Can run free through woods at Wallowbarrow
PARKING	Small car park at Seathwaite Parish Room (donations invited) and some spaces just north of church. Otherwise roadside parking at Point 5 (SD231975). Do not park near Newfield Inn while walking
PUBLIC TOILETS	None on route
NOTES	If River Duddon is in spate, not advisable to cross at Fickle Steps, Point 5. Return to Seathwaite along road instead

On loitering Muse – the swift Stream chides us – on!
Albeit his deep-worn channel doth immure
Objects immense portrayed in miniature,
Wild shapes for many a strange comparison!
Niagaras, Alpine passes and anon
Abodes of Naiads, calm abysses pure
Bright liquid mansions, fashioned to endure
When the broad oak drops a leafless skeleton,
And the solidities of mortal pride,
Palace and tower, are crumbled into dust! –
The Bard who talks with Duddon for his guide,
Shall find such toys of fancy thickly set:
Turn from the sight, enamoured muse we must;
And, if thou canst, leave them without regret!
William Wordsworth ('Hints for the Fancy from The River Duddon', 1820)

William Wordsworth loved the Duddon Valley so much that he wrote many such sonnets about it, and little has changed since his day. There's tarmac on those winding walled lanes, but the byres and woods and the lively stream that so enthralled the poet are still there for all to see. The walk begins in Seathwaite, a remote village set beneath the crags of Wallowbarrow. A reservoir service road takes the route easily up into the Coniston fells to the dam of Seathwaite Tarn. The large reservoir is dwarfed by the rocks of Grey Friar and Buzzard Crag towering above. On a windless day the crags are reflected to perfection in the hushed and gloomy waters. The view the other way is more spectacular, especially if the bracken glows red to blend with the dusky heather, the crags and the odd lonely pine. The jagged cone of Harter Fell dominates the skyline high above the forests, streams and farmhouses. This route descends through the heather and the bracken, and by a chattering beck to the Duddon. Over the road, it comes to the Fickle Steps across the river, with a wire to steady your progress. It's an exciting prelude to a wonderful walk through the Wallowbarrow Gorge. From a lofty path you look down on the river and it's tumbling waterfalls, then descend to a bouldery section, before a riverside stroll back into Seathwaite.

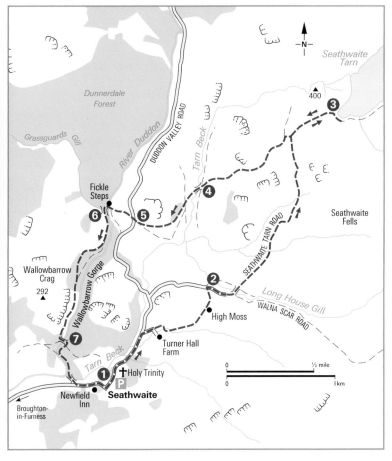

1. From Seathwaite, follow the road past the little church, then turn right on the tarmac lane towards Turner Hall Farm. Turn left through a gate marked 'High Moss'. Follow the track winding through level fields, pass left of some buildings and rise to a gate. Follow the field path under power lines out to the Walna Scar Road.

2. Turn right along the road. Where the tarmac ends, turn left over a bridge onto the access road to Seathwaite Tarn. This pleasant track climbs steadily to the reservoir dam.

3. Retrace your steps for around 450yds (411m) to a small waymarking post, highlighting a downhill path that weaves through rock and rough pasture to a gate by a sheepfold. A clearer track continues down to another gate, then across a boggy field. After another gate look for a ladder stile on the right.

4. Cross the stile and footbridge over Tarn Beck. On the opposite bank bear left and follow an obvious wet path through a gate and along the edge of a wood. Pass behind a cottage and continue past a barn on the left. The path swings right and rises to enter open country. Continue on this marshy way to the road.

5. Cross the road to a bridleway sign and follow the track to the Fickle Steps – huge boulders, with a wire handrail, which allow you to cross the River Duddon. (Caution: if the river is in spate here and the steps are underwater, return to the road, turn right and follow the road to Seathwaite.)

6. To continue on the route, turn left, cross a footbridge, turn right and then back left, tracing a tall deer fence. Climb to a high shoulder above the wooded Wallowbarrow Gorge before descending again to the bank of the River Duddon. Cross boulder-strewn terrain before the going eases and you reach a stone-arched bridge.

7. Cross the river and turn right, now following the eastern bank of the Duddon. When you meet a tributary, Tarn Beck, turn left, upstream, to a footbridge. Cross and walk out to the road. Turn left, and go through Seathwaite village, and back to the start.

Where to eat and drink

The Newfield Inn is a simply furnished but attractive pub, dating from the 17th century. There's a wood-burning stove in the bar and a wide range of real ales and tasty bar meals. A beer garden is in the back for fine days, and dogs are welcome.

What to see

You will see clumps of bog myrtle in the peat meadows of the Duddon Valley, especially near the end of the walk. It's a low aromatic shrub with woody stems and oval leaves, and it thrives in this boggy terrain. The branches have been used in past centuries, both for flavouring beer and for discouraging flies and midges, which apparently don't like its eucalyptus-like scent.

While you're there

Take a look around Broughton-in-Furness, a pleasant village near the Duddon Estuary. Chestnut trees surround the village square. Broughton's oldest building is the Church of St Mary Magdalene, which has Saxon walls and a Norman archway.

BROUGHTON TOWER AND THE FURNESS RAILWAY

DISTANCE/TIME	3.75 miles (6km) / 1hr 30min
ASCENT/GRADIENT	164ft (50m) / ▲ ▲
PATHS	Disused railway line, muddy tracks and field paths, 6 stiles
LANDSCAPE	Woods and fields
SUGGESTED MAP	OS Explorer OL6 The English Lakes (SW)
START/FINISH	Grid reference: SD212875
DOG FRIENDLINESS	Can be off lead for much of the walk
PARKING	In the Square at the centre of Broughton-in-Furness
PUBLIC TOILETS	On Knott Lane just north of the Square

Standing in the noble little square at the centre of Broughton-in-Furness, you may feel there was once some importance to this old Lancashire market town that seems to have since vanished. There are Georgian town houses and a fine obelisk commemorating the Golden Jubilee of George III. Close by you should spot the ancient fish slabs that once allowed the fishermen from Haverigg to lay out their catch, and the stocks, where the constable might detain petty thieves or swindlers. This Georgian heyday was a product of the local woodlands – swill basket making (baskets made from thin strips of woven oak) in particular – which, along with the early wood-based industrial processes for the locally occurring iron ore, ensured a prosperous bloom for what is still a fairly remote corner of Lakeland.

Furness Railway

In the 1850s the town became the fortuitous junction between an expanding Furness Railway, spreading out from the brand new industrial town of Barrow to the south, and the Whitehaven Railway from the north, bringing Lord Lowther's coal to Furness's ironworks. A branch line up the valley to Coniston's extensive copper mines quickly followed and for a brief period Broughton must have felt like it was at the fulcrum of the new industrial west. But industrial wealth is fickle, and little seemed to stick in Broughton itself. Broughton Tower, which had been given the 18th-century version of a garden makeover to create the fine parkland seen at the end of this walk, had additional wings attached to its 14th-century core.

The railway to Coniston fared little better. Mining traffic tailed off and the tourist trade became the mainstay, connecting with the Furness Railway's own pier and the steam yacht *Gondola*, plying its elegant way across Coniston Water. Amalgamation with the London, Midland and Scottish Railway in 1923, then nationalisation under British Railways in 1948, failed to address the decline in rail traffic though, and by 1958 it had gone the way of many rural branch lines. It closed for good in 1962 and the tracks were lifted the following year. The 21st century finds Broughton a quiet, attractive country town. The old railway line makes for a fine walking and cycling route, and Broughton Tower has been converted into executive flats. The Square is always busy and the town's market charter is still read out every year. The stocks however, remain unoccupied.

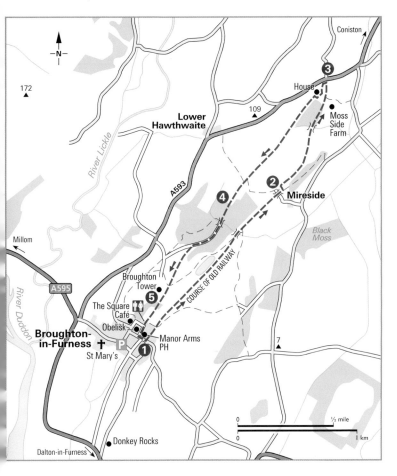

1. Leave the Square by the road beside the Manor Arms, Market Street. Walk down the left-hand side, passing a garage, to an opening on the left and a bridleway sign for Woodlands. Turn left here and join the trackbed of the former Coniston branch railway. Beyond a barrier, the path takes you through a cutting before crossing more open country. After about half a mile (800m) you'll find a tarn on the left with a bench. Continue for another half mile (800m) until you cross a bridge over a farm track.

2. Just beyond, look for a wicket gate on the left. Go through it, cross the farm track and pick out a gate on the opposite side. Take the enclosed path, raking upwards. Follow this through several gates, mostly uphill but with a few dips. The path tucks in around a wall on the right above Moss Side farm and

campsite. Beyond another gate the rising path, alongside a small beck, passes a treehouse before emerging almost at the main road (A593).

3. Don't go onto the main road, but turn immediately left down the access track to a house. Signposts direct you around the bottom of the garden and over a stile. Stay on the left-hand edge of the field beyond, cross a stile and follow a fence on the left until it turns a corner. A few paces further on, bear right on a green path hemmed in by gorse and bracken. Soon the path bears left to a step stile in a stone wall. Bear right to a grassy ridge marked by the remains of an old hedgerow. Maintain this direction past a stile then descend towards woodland. Crossing a dip you may find it easier to duck to the other side of the hedge to avoid a boggy patch. Rise to a stile by a sheepfold and continue with a hedge now on your left to the woods.

4. Go through the turnstile and descend to a gate and stile. Follow the right-hand edge of the next field to a wall gap, then follow the left-hand edge over a slight rise. Descend, soon bearing left through a gap in the trees along a green break. As the parkland opens out, aim for the left side of the wall encircling the grounds of Broughton Tower. Keep ahead around this boundary to a gate and turnstile into some woods.

5. Stay on this path past a children's playground and football pitch to reach a gate. Go through this and continue straight ahead to return to the Square.

Where to eat and drink

The Manor Arms is a good real ale pub, right on The Square, and serves hot snacks all day. Also on The Square is The Square Café, a friendly and unpretentious place that offers generous portions of cake.

What to see

Approaching Broughton Tower towards the end of the walk, you'll see the house itself is separated from its surrounding parkland by a low wall and ditch. This is known as a ha-ha, visible from the outside as an excluding wall sufficient to keep out most stock animals, but from the inside only noticeable when up close. In a time before lawnmowers, grazing sheep would be used to keep the ornamental grassland trimmed. The ha-ha prevented them straying into the flowerbeds and kitchen gardens closer to the house while maintaining the illusion of an uninterrupted sweep of countryside.

While you're there

A peculiar phenomenon on the southern edge of Broughton is the Donkey Rocks, in reality the exposed face of the old Eccleriggs Quarry. Here the dull red haematite that brought the Industrial Revolution to the Furness peninsula can be seen to good effect in the knobbly surface of a cliff 33ft (10m) high.

DUDDON BRIDGE AND THE SWINSIDE STONE CIRCLE

DISTANCE/TIME	6.6 miles (10.5km) / 2hrs 30min
ASCENT/GRADIENT	1,050ft (320m) / ▲ ▲
PATHS	Good paths (some can be muddy), farm roads, several stiles
LANDSCAPE	Wooded slopes, mostly rough pasture surrounded by hills
SUGGESTED MAP	OS Explorer OL6 The English Lakes (SW)
START/FINISH	Grid reference: SD197882
DOG FRIENDLINESS	On lead where sheep graze and on roads
PARKING	Parking space at Duddon Iron Furnace, near Duddon Bridge, or roadside spaces just to the north
PUBLIC TOILETS	None on route
NOTES	If Black Beck is in spate, stepping stones are uncrossable and the detour adds 0.75 miles (1.2km)

This is a peaceful walk in one of the quietest corners of the Lake District. It stretches from a tidal estuary to the flanks of the high fells, taking in old coppice woodlands and pastures where sheep and cattle are grazed. Blast furnaces and charcoal burners once belched smoke into the clean air, and ships laden with pig iron sailed from the narrow estuary, but that was a couple of centuries ago. Tucked away among the hills, and seldom visited, Swinside Stone Circle has stood over the scene for 4,000 years or more.

Duddon Iron Furnace

Dating from 1736, the Duddon Iron Furnace was one of eight rural blast furnaces in the area. Apart from the addition of an extra charcoal store, the structure has hardly changed since the day it was built. Information boards show the layout of the site, which included charcoal and iron ore stores, a wheelhouse, furnace, blowing house, casting house, office and slag heap. Ore and charcoal were fed into the furnace from the top of the site and pig iron left at the bottom. Ships transported the iron from Duddon Estuary to Bristol and Chepstow for use in the shipbuilding industry. The small rural furnaces simply went out of business when bigger blast furnaces were constructed. The ruins are managed by English Heritage and are always accessible.

Swinside Stone Circle

The lovely Swinside Stone Circle sits in a quiet hollow in the hills high above the estuary of the River Duddon. It is a late neolithic or early Bronze Age structure, with its stones closely packed together. It appears to be aligned on the midwinter solstice and is about 95ft (29m) in diameter. Locally it is called Sunkenkirk, from a legend relating how a church was once being built on the site, but the Devil kept pulling the stones down into the ground. Like many such circles around the country, it is also said that anyone counting the stones more than once will find that they arrive at a different number each time. With that in mind, it's probably best to say that there are more than 50, but fewer than 60 stones in the circle. There is also a series of standing stones near Ash House towards the end of the walk, but there is no public access to them.

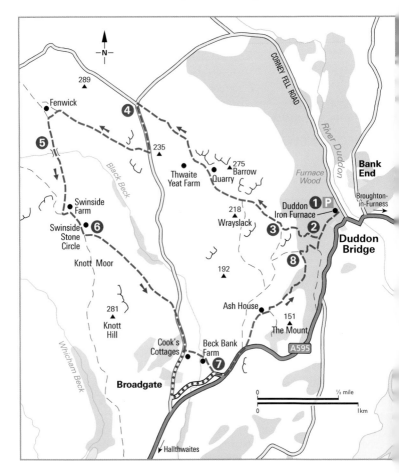

1. The Duddon Iron Furnace is on the left of the Corney Fell road, soon after the turning from Duddon Bridge. A public bridleway sign points up a track beside the ruins. By the last building, turn left up a woodland path marked by a low bridleway sign.

2. Cross a narrow access road and continue uphill. Turn right at a waymarked junction. The path is narrow and steep, but clear enough. Watch for a gate in a wall above on the left. Go through and follow a deep, narrow path flanked by bracken, crossing a low gap in the hills.

3. Meeting another track, bear right, and soon reach a gate. Go through and follow a walled track until it's crossed by a tall wall; go through the gate and

turn left. Follow a path roughly parallel to the wall and pass an old quarry. Traverse above a farm (Thwaite Yeat), keeping on a level course, then bear left, following traces of an old track, and ascend a moorland slope to a signpost at a road junction.

4. Turn left down a narrow road signposted 'Millom', and then turn right along a farm track. Follow this for 0.5 miles (800m) and go through a gate marked 'Fenwick'. Follow the track almost to the farm, then turn left at a public footpath sign. Cross three stiles as the path descends through fields to Black Beck.

5. Cross a footbridge and follow a vague path slanting up and left. Join a track near Swinside farm. Pass to the right of the buildings, then turn left to join and follow the access track downhill. Swinside Stone Circle is in a field on the left.

6. Walk down the access road, then bear right along a tarmac road to some cottages. Just before them is a stile and public footpath signpost; a field path and another stile lead to Black Beck. Go downstream to stepping stones leading to Beck Bank Farm. Follow waymarks through the farmyard and out to a road. (If the stones are uncrossable, retrace your steps to the cottages and turn left down the road, through Broadgate, to a T-junction. Turn left along the road past old mill buildings to rejoin the route at Point 7.)

7. Turn left along the road and left again along the A595. On a bend are two farm roads close together. Take the second one (by the postbox) to Ash House. Go straight and level through the garden to an iron gate. Go up to a stile, then right along a narrow path by a wall. Join a green track and continue into woods. Walk uphill, then down to reach a marker post at a junction.

8. Turn right and weave downhill, then keep left on a wider track. Cross a stream to meet the path used earlier. Descend this to retrace your steps to the Duddon Iron Furnace.

Where to eat and drink

The nearest pubs and cafés are at Broughton-in-Furness. On Princes Street, the Broughton Village Bakery and Café serves cake using flour from Cumbrian millers (open Monday to Saturday 9–1.45pm). Across the street, the Black Cock Inn is a friendly real ale pub serving tasty food at very reasonable prices.

What to see

Habitats range from estuary to woodland, and from lush pastures to moorland slopes. You can expect to find plenty of bird life, including curlews that are equally at home on the estuary and the high moorlands. Dippers frequent the rushing streams, while lapwings and skylarks are occasionally observed over the pastures. Treecreepers and nuthatches can be spotted in the woods, and buzzards may soar overhead.

While you're there

Just the other side of Broughton-in-Furness lies a very different landscape, the Duddon Mosses National Nature Reserve. A wild-looking wetland, it has been used by people for millennia, notably as a source of peat. It's a great place to see dragonflies, and if you go at dusk you may spot a barn owl silently hunting.

FROM ESKDALE TO MITERDALE

DISTANCE/TIME	6.75 miles (10.9km) / 4hrs
ASCENT/GRADIENT	1,312ft (400m) / ▲ ▲
PATHS	Good paths in valleys, but often indistinct on hills
LANDSCAPE	Heath and moor, with views across the surrounding valleys
SUGGESTED MAP	OS Explorer OL6 The English Lakes (SW)
START/FINISH	Grid reference: NY173007
DOG FRIENDLINESS	On lead as sheep roam moors
PARKING	Car park beside Dalegarth Station (pay-and-display)
PUBLIC TOILETS	At Dalegarth Station
NOTES	Walk not advised in poor visibility

Although William the Conqueror arrived in England in 1066, much of the North remained controlled by the Scots, and it was not until William II took Carlisle in 1092 that Norman influence spread through Lakeland. Some settlement was encouraged and land granted to found monastic houses, but much of the mountainous area remained undeveloped. The main reason for this lay in the Normans' almost fanatical devotion to the hunt, an activity exclusively reserved for the king and a few favoured subjects. Vast tracts of this northern 'wasteland' were 'afforested' – not in today's sense with the planting of trees, but rather set aside as wild game reserves and subject to special regulation, the Forest Law.

Noble hunting ground

The area around Eskdale lay within the barony of Copeland, a name which derives from the Old Norse *kaupaland* meaning 'bought land', and was granted to William de Briquessart in the early 12th century. His forest, together with the neighbouring Derwentfells Forest, extended all the way from the Esk to the Derwent and remained under Forest Law for more than a century. The forest was not devoid of settlement, but the few peasants who lived within its bounds were subject to many draconian laws that affected almost every aspect of their meagre existence. The clearance of additional land for grazing or cultivation, known as 'assarting', was forbidden and it was illegal to allow cattle or sheep to stray into the forest. Felling a tree for timber to repair a cottage or fencing required special permission, and even the collection of wood for fuel was strictly controlled. The estate was policed by foresters, who brought malefactors before the forest courts for judgement. The penalties were often severe, ranging from fines for minor infringements to flogging, mutilation or even death for poaching. Often near to starvation themselves, the commoners were required to assist as beaters, butchers and carriers for the hunts, and watch their overlords kill perhaps 100 deer in a single day. Yet if game animals broke through the fences around their allotments and destroyed the paltry crop, they were powerless to do anything more drastic than chase them away.

The hunting preserve gradually diminished during the 13th century, as larger areas were turned over to sheep farming. Constant nibbling has prevented the regeneration of natural woodland, leaving the open landscape now so characteristic of the area.

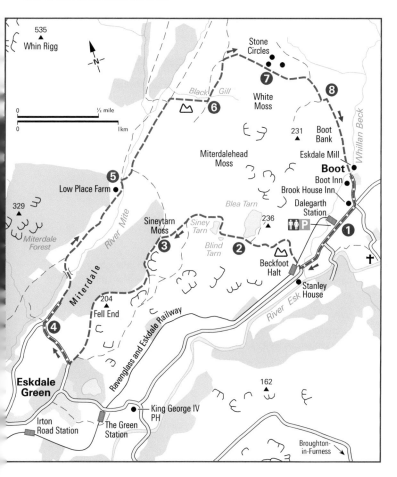

1. From the car park turn right down the valley road. At Beckfoot railway halt cross the line to a gate. A clear path starts by a wall then zig-zags up the hillside. Approaching Blea Tarn, go left, crossing a stream.

2. A few paces past a low tumbledown wall, fork right on a narrower path. This skirts right of Blind and Siney tarns. Keep left at a fork and pass a lone tree. Go left again before the slope drops away ahead. Pick the driest route across marshy ground, aiming for a wall around a conifer plantation.

3. Keep the wall on your right and reach a stile over a fence. Continue along the wall for another 0.75 miles (1.2km). As another wall converges, bear right to a gate in the corner and follow a short walled track to a junction. Another right turn takes you into Miterdale.

4. Turn right on a tarmac lane at the bottom of the track. Follow this and its stony continuation to a bridge over the River Mite, after which bear right and continue up the valley to Low Place Farm.

5. Walk past the farmhouse then take a gate on the right, signed 'Wasdale'. Walk upstream then cross a slightly hidden bridge to a track that continues along the opposite bank. Keep ahead for just under 0.75 miles (1.2km) before climbing more steeply to a gate at the far end of a cleared plantation. Immediately after, turn right and climb steeply beside the wall to a gate and stile at the top.

6. Bear left, cross a beck (Black Gill) and fork right, climbing gently over the moor. Pass a prominent boulder and follow the path bearing right across a slight dip to a couple of low stone circles.

7. Bear right at the second circle, and keep right past a wider circle and under a rocky outcrop. Go over a small rise then fork left on a vague path past a large cairn. A group of stone huts comes into view. Below these a clear track descends rightwards.

8. Follow the track down Boot Bank and into Boot. Cross Whillan Beck by Eskdale Mill to continue through the village. At the end turn right to Dalegarth Station and the start of your walk.

Where to eat and drink

The Fellbites Café at Dalegarth station serves hot and cold drinks, sandwiches and cakes. If you want something more substantial, call at either the Boot Inn or the Brook House Inn in Boot.

What to see

Scattered across Brat's Moss are the remains of stone huts and a field system, as well as five impressive circles of standing stones. They were erected during the Bronze Age, perhaps 5,500 years ago, and suggest quite a large settlement on what is now an almost desolate landscape.

While you're there

The Eskdale Watermill still stands beside the packhorse bridge in Boot. It was built to grind corn in 1578 and worked by successive generations of the same family for almost 350 years.

AROUND BUTTERMERE

DISTANCE/TIME	4.5 miles (7.2km) / 2hrs
ASCENT/GRADIENT	310ft (95m) / ▲
PATHS	Good paths, some road walking
LANDSCAPE	Lake, fells, woodland and farmland
SUGGESTED MAP	OS Explorer OL4 The English Lakes (NW)
START/FINISH	Grid reference: NY173169
DOG FRIENDLINESS	On lead near farms and open fells where sheep are grazing
PARKING	Car park beyond the Buttermere Court Hotel (fee)
PUBLIC TOILETS	At start

Much has been written about Buttermere, the dale, the village and the lake; it remains, as it has been since Victorian times, a popular place displaying 'nature's art for art's sake', as W G Collingwood described it in *The Lake Counties* (1902). Nicholas Size's historical romance, *The Secret Valley* (1930), takes a rather different and much earlier line, describing a tale of guerrilla warfare and bloody battles here with invading Norman forces (see Walk 44).

The Maid of Buttermere

Buttermere achieved considerable notoriety at the pen of Joseph Budworth, who stayed here in 1792 and encountered Mary, the daughter of the landlord of the Fish Inn (now the Buttermere Court Hotel). In his guidebook *Fortnight's Ramble to the Lakes*, he describes Mary as 'the reigning Lily of the Valley' and began what must have been a reign of terror for Mary, who became a tourist attraction, a situation made worse in later editions of Budworth's book, in which he revelled in the discomfort all the unwanted attention heaped on Mary and her family.

More sinisterly, in 1802, the tale brought to Buttermere one John Hadfield, a man posing as the Honourable Anthony Augustus Hope MP. Hadfield wooed and won Mary, and they were married at Lorton church on 2 October 1802 (coincidentally just two days before William Wordsworth married Mary Hutchinson). With the honeymoon scarcely begun, Hadfield was exposed as an impostor, and arrested on a charge of forgery – a more serious offence than of bigamy, of which he was also guilty – and later tried and hanged at Carlisle. Accounts of the whole episode are given by Thomas de Quincey in *Recollections of the Lakes and the Lake Poets* and by Melvyn Bragg in his 1987 novel *The Maid of Buttermere*, a description used by Wordsworth in 'The Prelude'. The whole saga was dramatised and found its way onto the stages of some London theatres. Happily for Mary, she later remarried, had a large family and by all accounts a happy life.

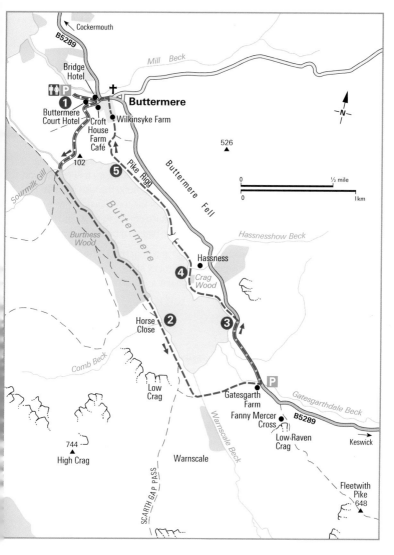

1. Leave the car park and turn right, passing the Buttermere Court Hotel to follow a broad track through gates. Ignore the signposted route to Scale Force and continue along the track towards the edge of the lake, then follow the line of a hedgerow, right, to a bridge at Buttermere Dubs. Cross a second, smaller footbridge and go through a gate in the wall at the foot of Burtness Wood and the cascade of Sourmilk Gill. Turn left on a track through the woodland that roughly parallels the lakeshore. Keep left at any forks to stay close to the water's edge. You finally emerge from the woods via a gate near Horse Close, where a bridge spans Comb Beck.

2. Keep on along the lower path to reach a meeting of walls. Go left through the gate, cross Warnscale Beck and walk out to Gatesgarth Farm. Walk along

the fenced path to the left of the farmyard to reach the valley road. A short stretch of road walking, left on the B5289, now follows, along which there are no pathways. Be careful of approaching traffic.

3. As the road bends left, leave it for a lakeside footpath on the left. The path leads into a field, beyond which it never strays far from the shoreline, and continues to a stand of Scots pine near Crag Wood.

4. Beyond Hassnesshow Beck bridge, the path enters the grounds of Hassness, where a gate leads to a rocky path enclosed by trees. Here a path has been cut across a crag where it plunges into the lake below, and shortly disappears into a brief, low and damp tunnel, the only one of its kind in the Lake District. The tunnel was cut by employees of George Benson, a 19th-century mill owner who owned the Hassness Estate, so that he could walk around the lake without straying far from its shore. After you emerge from the tunnel a gate gives access to a gravel path across the wooded pasture of Pike Rigg. A path leads through a series of gates beyond the foot of the lake to a bridge of slate slabs.

5. At the foot of the lake, keep straight ahead at a fingerpost. After a bridge of slate slabs, the path bends right, up some rocky steps, and then left to Wilkinsyke Farm. Continue to the road. Turn left and left again beside the Bridge Hotel to return to the car park.

Where to eat and drink

There are two hotels in Buttermere, the Bridge Hotel and Buttermere Court Hotel. Both hotels serve food and drink seven days a week and both have small outdoor areas that are great for an al fresco meal on a warm summer's day. Alternatively try the Croft House Farm café, opposite the Bridge Hotel, for hot drinks and light snacks, either eat in or take away.

What to see

While walking out to Gatesgarth Farm, look over to the craggy sides of Fleetwith Pike. On the lower slopes a white cross can be seen. This was erected by the friends of Fanny Mercer, a visitor to Lakeland in 1887, who tripped over her walking pole and fell to her death.

While you're there

Walk up the road to Buttermere's attractive church (1841), set in a superb position on a rocky knoll. It is tiny, one of the smallest in Lakeland, with a bellcote and a lower chancel. From it there is a lovely view of the valley and the high fells on the south side, all the way to Hay Stacks.

44

A CLIMB UP RANNERDALE KNOTTS

DISTANCE/TIME	2.9 miles (4.7km) / 2hrs
ASCENT/GRADIENT	837ft (255m) / ▲ ▲ ▲
PATHS	Steep rocky paths, grassy paths and tracks
LANDSCAPE	Steep fellside, open fell, valley and lake
SUGGESTED MAP	OS Explorer OL4 The English Lakes (NW)
START/FINISH	Grid reference: NY163183
DOG FRIENDLINESS	Sheep grazing – keep dogs on lead throughout
PARKING	Roadside layby near start
PUBLIC TOILETS	None on route

This peculiar little mountain is worth the effort at most times of the year. The rugged face it sets against the valley of Crummock Water looks unassailable until you find the key, a winding staircase of grass and rock steps, breaching its craggy summit after only a relatively short burst of exertion. Even in low cloud this creates an exhilarating experience of loftiness. On clear days the view is nothing short of magnificent. Crummock Water's depths below the end of Rannerdale's crags plunge to over 70ft (21.3m) barely 8ft (2.4m) from the road. Little wonder then that in former times folk chose a route to Buttermere over the shoulder of this fell, steering clear of those terrifying underwater depths. The modern car required a more level approach, and so the lakeside road was blasted out of the rock.

Nicholas Size

The road disarms Rannerdale Knotts of its most dramatic power – that of a barrier to the secret valley of Buttermere beyond. This at least was the theory developed by Nicholas Size (1866–1953), who once ran the Buttermere (now the Bridge) Hotel in the village. Size, a former railwayman, forsook his life as the goods manager at the old Bradford Exchange Station to become an outspoken proponent of tourist 'development' in the valley. A man of many schemes, one such was to open a nine hole golf course on the meadows between Buttermere and Crummock Water, and another involved a cable car up to High Crag.

Secret Valley

Size is not remembered by posterity as an eccentric hotelier, however, but as an author. He was captivated by the absence of historical records about the area, particularly before the Normans exerted effective control in the 12th century. There were folk tales, and of course the place-names, with their Norse and Celtic origins. Size set about putting some flesh on the stories and in *The Secret Valley* (1930) created a historical novella using the backdrop of his valley as a storyline. Earl Bothar, the last of the Celtic warrior chiefs, defends his homeland from Norman invaders, coming up the dale from their castle at

Cockermouth. Faced with the barrier of Rannerdale Knotts, the British lure their attackers into the dead-end valley to the north, before descending on them from the surrounding heights in a massacre. It's gripping stuff, and the book sold in vast quantities to a 1930s public keen to read of resistance to foreign invaders. The bluebells that flourish on Rannerdale's open fellsides are supposed to have grown up from the corpses of the Norman invaders.

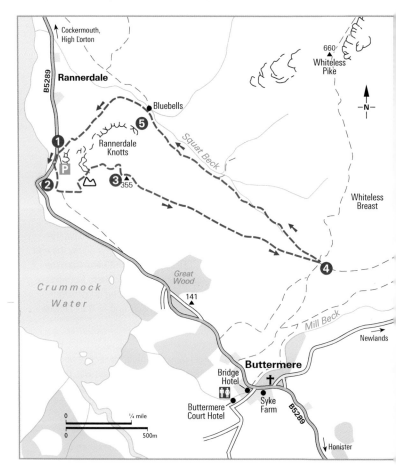

1. With your back to the parking area turn left along the road for a few paces to a footpath sign on the left. Here you'll find a steep, pitched path that begins a snaking ascent of the precipitous slope.

2. Keep to the clearest path, which swings left and climbs through the bracken. On reaching a knoll, you're treated to views of Buttermere and Crummock Water in the valley below. The path zig-zags back to the left now. At the top of a short rise, keep to the right of a small pile of slate, ignoring the inviting, grassy path and instead climb a stony trail that quickly becomes a flight of rocky steps through a rocky ravine. As the grassy slopes return you are confronted by a pair of crags looming ahead. Your upward path is deflected to the

right, emerging on a grassy shoulder before bearing right to the summit. The slightly underwhelming highest point is made worthwhile by taking a few paces towards the edge to reveal a magnificent vista up and down the valley.

3. Follow the obvious ridge path, which includes one awkward rocky section before settling down to become an airy high-level route across a series of bracken-coated grassy knolls. As you approach the final humps, a short cut drops down to the left, but completists will want to carry on to the end of the ridge, where it terminates at a grassy crossing of paths above the valley of Mill Beck beneath Whiteless Breast.

4. Turn left and immediately left again down the valley path that now mirrors your high-level outward journey. Follow the path all the way down to a gate near a wall corner by a footbridge.

5. In spring it's worth crossing here to immerse yourself in the fellside bluebells, however, please observe any National Trust path signs to avoid damaging the wild flowers. At other times of the year, continue with the water on your right on a path that clings to the foot of the fell. This soon swerves left away from the beck. When faced with any choices, keep left to stay close to the base of the rocky slope. Pass through a kissing gate and continue with a wall now on your right to emerge at the back of the little parking area.

Where to eat and drink

There's a good choice at Buttermere village including the Bridge Hotel (Nicholas Size's 'Buttermere Hotel') and the Buttermere Court Hotel. Syke Farm produces its own delicious ice cream and boasts a delightful, rustic café space.

What to see

In May, Rannerdale is famous for its bluebells. These delightful woodland flowers grow in super abundance on the bare fellside, an incongruity that clearly inspired generations of storytellers. The truth is more prosaic. The fellside here was probably still wooded until the 18th century and the plants are a hangover from those days.

While you're there

Drive up the Whinlatter Pass from High Lorton to visit the Whinlatter Forest Visitor Centre. There's a splendid shop and café, as well as an interpretive centre and displays about the forest's resident ospreys. There's a good children's play area too, along with bike hire, mountain bike trails and a Go-Ape high ropes course (see Walk 35).

A LOWESWATER LOOP

45

DISTANCE/TIME	5.5 miles (8.8km) / 3hrs 15min
ASCENT/GRADIENT	774ft (236m) / ▲
PATHS	Well-defined paths and tracks, all stiles have adjacent gates
LANDSCAPE	Hillside, farm pastures, forest and lakes
SUGGESTED MAP	OS Explorer OL4 The English Lakes (NW)
START/FINISH	Grid reference: NY134210
DOG FRIENDLINESS	On lead, except for Holme Wood
PARKING	Maggie's Bridge car park, Loweswater (get there early)
PUBLIC TOILETS	None on route

Loweswater is one of Lakeland's finest yet least talked about lakes – perhaps because it's a bit remote from the more popular parts of Lakeland. Beyond Buttermere and Crummock Water, most people never quite get around to visiting it; possibly they're just awed by the beauty of the other lakes. The fellwalker judges Lakeland by the height of the fells, and the fells here are low – one's even called Low Fell. But somehow, standing on the lakeshore, it doesn't matter.

Loweswater's a bit of a thief: it steals the best views of Crummock Water's fells. Grasmoor and Whiteside never looked more fair than they do from Carling Knott's balcony path, and little Mellbreak bursts into the sky like a volcano.

Following the corpse road

Loweswater village is little more than the Kirkstile Inn, the church and the village hall, with a scattering of whitewashed farm buildings in the lush green fields and alongside the narrow country lanes. The walk starts on the outskirts of the village by Maggie's Bridge, and uses an old corpse road to get to the fellsides. The corpses would have been parishioners from Loweswater, for the church didn't have its own burial ground – they would be strapped onto horses' backs before being carried all the way to St Bees on the coast. After the climb up the high sides of Carling Knott, the mourners might not have appreciated that this is one of the most splendid balcony paths in Cumbria – green, flat and true, and with wonderful views across the lake to Darling Fell.

To farmland and lake

The old track descends to farm pastures. The names of the farmhouses – Iredale Place, Jenkinson Place and Hudson Place – are all derived from the original owners' names. Beyond the latter, the route drops to the lake. Loweswater is celebrated among anglers for its trout and its perch. Both fish are hunted down by the predatory pike, a huge streamlined fish present here in large numbers. The path continues into the National Trust's Holme

Wood. Oak predominates near the lake, although the trees at the top of the wood largely consist of pine, larch and Sitka spruce. The wood is one of the last strongholds of the red squirrel. You're very likely to see pied and spotted flycatchers here, and maybe, if you're lucky, a green woodpecker. The path leaves the lake behind, comes out of the woods and crosses the fields of Watergate, back to Maggie's Bridge. Mellbreak still towers above the trees, tauntingly, tantalisingly showing off its scree paths to the summit – perhaps a walk for another day.

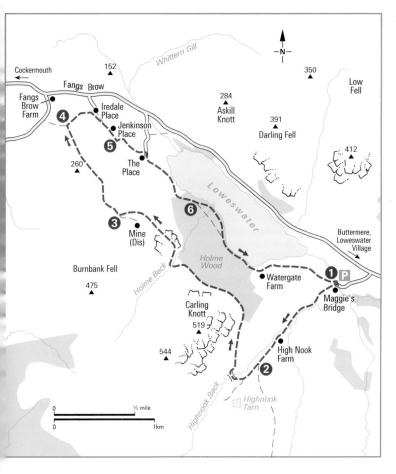

1. Just opposite the car park entrance, go through the gate to High Nook Farm and follow the track through the fields. After passing through the farmyard bear left along a stony track that climbs towards the comb of Highnook Beck and the craggy sides of Carling Knott.

2. After a gate take the right fork each time the path divides. This will bring you down to the footbridge over Highnook Beck. Once across, the route continues as a fine grassy track that doubles back right, raking across the hillside to the top of the Holme Wood plantations. The track follows the top edge of the woods before traversing the breast of Burnbank Fell.

3. The track swings left and climbs to reach a ladder stile and a gate to the north of the fell. Go over the stile and descend gradually northwest across high pastureland.

4. A couple of hundred yards short of the road, at Fangs Brow, turn right over a ladder stile and then continue along a track above Iredale Place farm. At the junction near the house, bear right to join a tarmac lane.

5. At Jenkinson Place the tarmac lane ends. Continue ahead and through a gate. Swing slightly left, down a faint, grassy track leading to a gate in the wall on the other side of the field. Go through this and follow the line of trees. Beyond the next gate, aim for the buildings of The Place. Just before reaching them, a gate on the left leads on to a faint path beside a wall and fence on the right. Turn right and follow the lane, which becomes a track near the shores of Loweswater before entering Holme Wood.

6. A wide track now heads through the woods, but by taking a clear gravel path to the left you can get nearer the shoreline. This second path rejoins the original track just beyond a stone-built bunkhouse. At Watergate Farm, turn left to follow a wide gravel road back to the car park at Maggie's Bridge.

Where to eat and drink

The Kirkstile Inn at Loweswater is one of the best in the Lakes. It serves excellent, locally sourced food complemented by an extensive but reasonably priced wine list. Dogs are welcomed in the bar but not in the restaurant. Oak-beamed ceilings and an open fire make this an inviting place after a day on the hills.

What to see

One thing you may notice on your visit to Loweswater is that it outflows not to the lowlands, but towards the high fells – the only lake in Cumbria to do this. You'll see the stream at Maggie's Bridge, from where it flows beneath Mellbreak's northern slopes into Crummock Water. In the last glacial period, the great ice sheets of the Irish Sea and the high fells collided, leaving deep deposits of glacial debris that blocked Loweswater's northwestern shores.

While you're there

There's been a place of worship at Loweswater since 1158, when Ranulph de Lyndesay gave some land and a chapel to the Abbey of St Bees. In 1827 that building was demolished to make way for the present much larger church, since lead mining had increased the local population to over 500 at this time. At the same time a school for 80 children was built – it's now the village hall.

NETHER WASDALE TO WAST WATER

DISTANCE/TIME	4.5 miles (7.2km) / 2hrs
ASCENT/GRADIENT	165ft (50m) / ▲
PATHS	Well-defined paths and farm tracks
LANDSCAPE	Farm pasture, deciduous woodland, low moor
SUGGESTED MAP	OS Explorer OL6 The English Lakes (SW)
START/FINISH	Grid reference: NY127038
DOG FRIENDLINESS	Can run free in Low Wood; on lead elsewhere
PARKING	Car park in the woods, just north of Forest Bridge
PUBLIC TOILETS	None on route

If you're driving past Nether Wasdale, the chances are you're on the way to Wasdale Head and thinking about the climb to Great Gable, or England's highest mountain, Scafell Pike. Nether Wasdale and its surrounding oak woods are pretty, but these narrow, twisting lanes and their enclosing stone walls make you concentrate on your driving. The area is too good to be dismissed, however. Delightful paths through those oak woods lead to Wast Water, where you can look across to the vast rock screes that fan out from Whin Rigg.

Cold and clear

As lakes go, Wast Water is fairly sterile. When water tumbles down the impervious volcanic rocks of the surrounding mountains, few of the minerals needed for a rich cycle of life are leached out into the lake. You'll see some black-headed gulls and maybe the occasional red-breasted merganser, but the most fascinating visitor to Wast Water is a fish. The Arctic char comes here to spawn in the lake's ice-cold waters each year between November and March, and has been doing so since the last ice age.

The great fans of stone known as the Wastwater Screes fall from the crags of Whin Rigg and Illgill Head, continuing down far below the water surface. Wast Water is England's deepest lake at 258ft (79m). Its depth and its clear waters make it popular with scuba divers.

The view of the mountains around the head of the lake was once voted 'Britain's Favourite View' by the public. This view, with Great Gable at its centre, is also the basis for the Lake District National Park logo. The classic viewpoint is a little further up the lake than this walk reaches, but you get a very good approximation when you climb up to the road after passing Wasdale Hall. This point is also directly opposite the highest fan of scree. You can tell that the mountainside is still shedding rock regularly as the scree is almost devoid of vegetation.

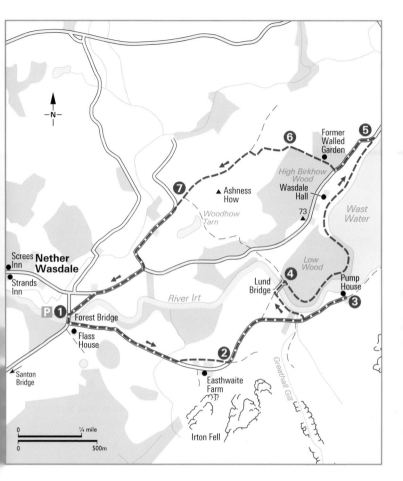

1. From the car park exit to the road and turn right. Cross the River Irt on a stone bridge, then turn left immediately on a stony track. The track leads through fields to Easthwaite Farm; skirt left around it on a secondary track, rejoining the main track just beyond.

2. Continue along the track through more fields, now tucked beneath the rocks of Irton Fell. After a slight descent, the track comes close to the River Irt then reaches the Wast Water Pump House at the foot of Wast Water. Water from the lake is pumped from here to Sellafield nuclear plant at Seascale.

3. Beyond the pumphouse a narrow, undulating path follows the lakeshore to reach the foot of the Screes. You may wish to continue a little further just to get a feel for it, but then retrace your steps, past the pump house, to a little gate on the right leading to a narrow riverside path. Follow this by the Irt to Lund Bridge and cross over.

4. Go through a kissing gate then keep right on a clear path parallel to the river. This winds through Low Wood, bends left behind a little boathouse and continues along the lakeshore. The path approaches Wasdale Hall, a

161

magnificent mansion now used as a youth hostel. Ignore branching paths to the hall and stay on the main lakeside path until it climbs slightly to a gate. Just above this you meet the Wasdale Head road. Here, you get a grand view over the lake towards the Screes, Yewbarrow and Great Gable.

5. Turn left along the road then, after about 300yds (274m), turn right along a wide stony track with a footpath sign. Follow this between High Birkhow Woods and Wasdale Hall's long-abandoned walled gardens. Go over a stile at the end of the track to enter high pastures with the crags of Buckbarrow and Middle Fell away to the right.

6. The path begins as a faint grooved track, heading half left over a slight rise then bending back right towards a low rocky outcrop. From here it becomes well defined and winds downhill to meet another track at a T-junction. Turn left along this track, which aims southwest with the rocks of Ashness How to your left. When you see footpath waymarks to the left, you could make a short there-and-back detour to see Woodhow Tarn.

7. Otherwise continue straight ahead. Ignore another bridleway going right and follow the track ahead. It passes a cottage before veering left to the Nether Wasdale road. Turn right and then fork left (signed Santon Bridge). At the next junction the car park is a short way to the right.

Where to eat and drink
The welcoming Strands Inn in Nether Wasdale is a typical English country inn with low beams and a real fire to warm you on a winter's evening. Opposite the Strands Inn is the Screes Inn, a sister to The Strands Inn, both serve fine ales and food. A microbrewery has been onsite, since 2007, earning several national awards for its beer.

What to see
Peregrines nest on the precipitous crags around Buckbarrow. This medium-sized falcon is distinctive, its wingtops and upper body flecked with various shades of grey. Its cheeks are white, and its lower body pale with dark grey streaks. The peregrine's incredible eyesight allows it to see prey from 2 miles (3.2km) away. When it finds something, the bird dives ('stoops') at great speed from the sky; with recorded speeds in excess of 200mph (320km/h), it is generally reckoned to be the fastest living thing on Earth.

While you're there
Take a look round Gosforth village. In St Mary's churchyard is an interesting 14ft (4m) stone cross dating from the 10th century, the highest of its kind in England. The cross has pagan Viking symbols on one side and Christian engravings on the other.

CLIMBING BLACK COMBE

DISTANCE/TIME	8.5 miles (13.7km) / 4hrs
ASCENT/GRADIENT	2,001ft (610m) / ▲ ▲ ▲
PATHS	Clear path to top, indistinct at start of descent; two significant fords on return route
LANDSCAPE	Broad, open, whaleback hill covered in bracken and heather
SUGGESTED MAP	OS Explorer OL6 The English Lakes (SW)
START/FINISH	Grid reference: SD136827
DOG FRIENDLINESS	On lead or under close control throughout
PARKING	Car park at Whicham church (with honesty box) or layby at Whitbeck church
PUBLIC TOILETS	None on route
NOTES	Not advised in poor visibility

Black Combe truly dominates this quiet corner of the Lake District. Its steep slopes rise to a domed summit (1,968ft/600m) that often wears a woolly cap of cloud. Moist air rising from the Irish Sea has to cross Black Combe before reaching the higher fells, so tends to leave a puffy cloud tethered to the summit as water vapour starts to condense. Bear this in mind when attempting the climb; the whole idea is to enjoy the view from Lakeland's last fell and cloud cover will confound the plan. Also bear in mind that this is one of the higher and more remote walks in this book. Black Combe is not a place to be caught out in foul weather.

William Wordsworth commented on the view from Black Combe, claiming that 'the amplest range of unobstructed prospect may be seen that British ground commands' though lamenting, 'we have seen into Scotland, Wales, the Isle of Man but alas we have still failed to see Ireland.' Come on a clear day and you may have better luck.

Black Combe is made of friable Skiddaw slate, which outcrops around Skiddaw and also on the Isle of Man. It is the oldest exposed rock in the Lake District, belonging to the Ordovician period of 450–500 million years ago, and weathers to produce domed summits covered in patchy scree and thin, poor soil. Bracken covers the lower slopes of the fell, giving way to bilberry and heather on the higher slopes, though the summit is a delightful swathe of short green grass. Tree cover is sparse and confined to the lower slopes. Grouse, introduced for sport, flourish on the slopes along with snipe and curlew. Several streams have carved deep little valleys in the flanks of Black Combe. Millergill Beck was once used to turn a waterwheel at Whitbeck Mill. The present building, restored as a dwelling, dates from the 18th century; the dilapidated wheel last turned in 1916. Too many old farms and cottages lie derelict or disused on the flanks of the hill, victims of wavering farm economies, and Black Combe is one large sheep-grazing range today.

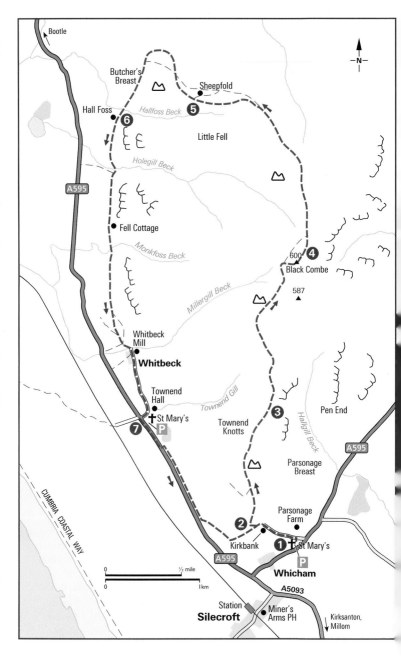

1. From the car park at Whicham church, walk along the walled path between the church and the old school to a lane. Turn left to walk up behind Kirkbank. At a bridleway sign, turn right onto the open fell.

2. The fellside is covered in bracken, but a broad, grassy path leads straight up a little valley. Avoid a path climbing steeply to the left. Towards the top of the

valley, bracken gives way to grass and bilberry. Behind you, coastal views are developing nicely, stretching beyond Millom to the Furness Peninsula.

3. The broad path becomes stony as it slants left across a heathery slope. Nearing the summit, the high fells of the central Lake District appear ahead. Ignoring the faint path continuing straight on, follow the clearer route that bends sharp right for the final pull to the broad, domed top of Black Combe. A trig point is enclosed by a circular wall.

4. You can turn around and retrace your steps to Whicham, or enjoy a fine circuit around the fell. Head northeast from the summit and you'll soon pick up a reasonably clear path heading in your direction. Follow this for about 250yds (230m) and then turn left along a narrow, grassy trail that broadens as it descends.

5. Descend to a broad heather-clad shoulder. The path swings left near an old sheepfold, then back right. The village of Bootle soon comes into view. At a fork, ignore the path dropping left (it gets too steep) and keep straight on. The path later swings left and continues down beside a fence on Butcher's Breast, then runs by a wall, fords Hallfoss Beck and passes close to the ruined farm of Hall Foss.

6. Keep to the path beside the wall, fording Holegill Beck near a solitary larch. Pass abandoned Fell Cottage and cross Monkfoss Beck on a little bridge. When a fork is reached, keep left to follow a grassy path across a slope of bracken. A track leads past Whitbeck Mill, then passes scattered cottages before meeting the main road (A595) at Whitbeck church.

7. Turn left through a layby and go along the verge. At a footpath sign to Black Combe, go up the path a few paces then branch right on a path just above the road. Eventually it climbs away from the road and forks. Bear left here, later walking beside a wall. Continue along a track, soon passing the bridleway sign above Kirkbank. Retrace your route to the car park.

Where to eat and drink
The Miner's Arms near Silecroft station is the nearest pub, but isn't open on a Monday or Tuesday. There are also choices in Kirksanton and Millom to the south, and Bootle to the north.

What to see
In crystal-clear conditions the panorama embraces the higher Lakeland fells, the Yorkshire Dales, Bowland, Snowdonia, the Isle of Man and the Galloway Hills in Scotland. If Ireland can be seen, it will be a hazy portion of the Antrim plateau or the dim bumps of the Mountains of Mourne.

While you're there
If you can spare the time, visit the Millom Heritage and Arts Centre, a little museum that's crammed full of bits and bobs associated with the town and local area from the Bronze Age through to World War II.

OVER MUNCASTER FELL FROM RAVENGLASS

DISTANCE/TIME	6 miles (9.7km) / 2hrs 30min
ASCENT/GRADIENT	730ft (223m) / ▲ ▲
PATHS	Clear tracks and paths, muddy in places
LANDSCAPE	Woodlands, moderately rugged fell and gentle valley
SUGGESTED MAP	OS Explorer OL6 The English Lakes (SW)
START	Grid reference: SD085964
FINISH	Grid reference: SD145998
DOG FRIENDLINESS	Under close control where sheep are grazing
PARKING	Village car park at Ravenglass, close to station
PUBLIC TOILETS	Near the car park at Ravenglass station

Muncaster Fell is a long and knobbly fell of no great height. The summit rises to 758ft (231m), but is a little off the route described. A winding path negotiates the fell from end to end and this can be linked with other paths and tracks to offer a fine walk from Ravenglass to Eskdale Green. It's a linear walk, but when the Ravenglass and Eskdale Railway is in full steam, a ride back on the train is simply a joy.

Affectionately known as La'al Ratty, the Ravenglass and Eskdale Railway has a history of fits and starts. It was originally opened as a standard gauge track in 1875 to serve a granite quarry and was converted to narrow gauge between 1915 and 1917. After a period of closure it was bought by enthusiasts in 1960, overhauled and re-opened, and is now a firm favourite for visitors. The line runs from Ravenglass to Dalegarth station, near Boot, at the head of Eskdale. The railway runs daily from mid-March to October, plus selected days in winter – check the timetable for details.

The Romans operated an important port facility at Ravenglass. Fortifications were built all the way around the Cumbrian coast to link with Hadrian's Wall and a Roman road cut through Eskdale, over the passes to Ambleside, then along the crest of High Street to link with the road network near Penrith. Some people think the Romans planned to invade Ireland from Ravenglass, though this is a subject of debate. The mainline railway sliced through the old Roman fort in 1850, leaving only the bathhouse intact, though even this ruin is among the tallest Roman remains in Britain. The Romans also operated a tileworks on the lower slopes of Muncaster Fell.

Surrounded by luxuriant rhododendrons, Muncaster Castle is almost completely hidden from view. It has been the home of the Pennington family since about 1240, though they occupied a nearby site even earlier than that. The estate around the castle includes a church that was founded in 1170, as well as a network of paths and tracks to explore. Owls are bred and reared at Muncaster, then released into the wild.

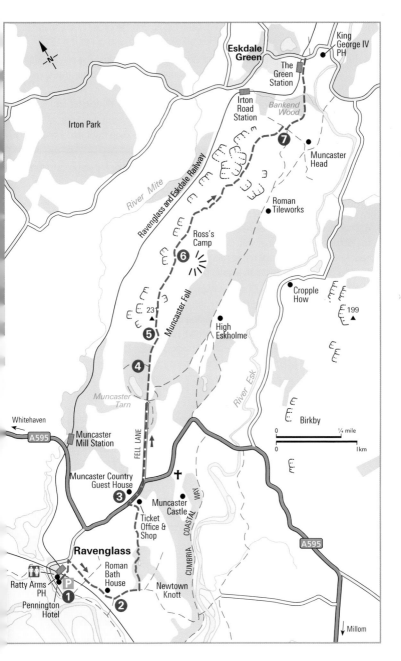

1. Leave the car park by the footbridge over the railway lines, then follow the path to a road. Turn right, signposted 'Roman Bath House'. Pass a campsite, then use a footpath alongside the lane to reach the Roman bathhouse.

2. Continue along the access lane then fork left on a track signposted 'Esk Tr'. Turn left again before houses and follow another track up a little wooded

valley. Pass a little lake then walk between fields. Enter another wood, then turn left by the Muncaster Castle ticket office and shop, and out to the A595.

3. Turn right along the road, changing sides near a phone box. The road leads up to a bend, where Fell Lane is signposted uphill. Ascend the clear track, cross a little wooded dip, then fork right and left, noticing Muncaster Tarn on the left. Go up then through a gate and soon emerge onto Muncaster Fell.

4. Walk alongside a plantation of conifers on your left. Where this ends, a path rising to the left leads to the summit – otherwise keep right to continue on the walk.

5. There are several possible paths now, but the best route for views is to fork left on a rising path about 200 yards (183m) beyond the end of the plantation. Follow the main path along the ridge. This arrives at a steep little descent overlooking a broad boggy area, where alternative routes reunite.

6. Drop down and loop leftward around the boggy area to reach a gateway at the corner of a dry-stone wall. Descend parallel to the wall then cross a broad saddle to a built-up track rising round the right side of a knoll. Follow the drier track winding down, through a gate in a wall and round a final knoll (Rabbit How) to a crossing track.

7. Go through the gate and then turn left across the field, past a large boulder, to a wall enclosing trees. Bear right along the wall, then keep it on your left through the next field, which funnels down to a ford with stepping stones; a narrow track continues. Where another track crosses your path, find The Green station at Eskdale Green just above.

Where to eat and drink
The Ratty Arms at Ravenglass station serves good-value bar meals. In the village, the Pennington Hotel also welcomes families and serves meals. The King George IV, near The Green station, is a very walker-friendly pub with good food and beer.

What to see
The Ravenglass Estuary is a haunt of wildfowl and waders. Oystercatchers and curlews probe the mudflats and there are sometimes raucous gulls. On Muncaster Fell there may be grouse in the heather and it's usual to see buzzards overhead.

While you're there
Explore the little village of Ravenglass, originally a fishing village at the confluence of the rivers Irt, Mite and Esk. Apart from being a Roman port, by 1280 it had charters for a weekly market and annual fair, although its trade was eclipsed as the port of Whitehaven developed and it became a rum-smuggling centre.

NANNYCATCH BECK AND ITS VALLEY

DISTANCE/TIME	9.5 miles (15.3km) / 5hrs
ASCENT/GRADIENT	1,508ft (460m) / ▲ ▲ ▲
PATHS	Well-defined paths and farm tracks, 4 stiles
LANDSCAPE	Lake and riverside pastures, forest and moorland
SUGGESTED MAP	OS Explorer 303 Whitehaven & Workington and OS Explorer OL4 The English Lakes (NW)
START/FINISH	Grid reference: NY012130
DOG FRIENDLINESS	Can run free through forest
PARKING	Free car park at Longlands Lake, Cleator
PUBLIC TOILETS	None on route

Cleator, Cleator Moor, Frizington and Rowrah are all rather gloomy places with rows of 19th-century terraced housing and telephone wires dangling across the street. This is where the last hills of Cumbria decline to the Ehen Valley, and, as forestry cloaks the slopes, it looks as though there's nothing to keep the walker here. Yet those who've done Alfred Wainwright's Coast to Coast walk, from nearby St Bees to Robin Hood's Bay in North Yorkshire, know different. They've seen what lies beyond the first hill; the hidden valley and the clear, crystal stream that dances through it. They've seen Nannycatch.

Before the 1780s Cleator Moor was just that – a moor, untouched and windswept. But not far beneath those grasses were veins rich in haematite, a red iron ore, and the growing need for high-quality iron started a rush to equal that of the Klondyke. The Longlands Mine at Cleator first produced iron ore in 1879. Flooding from the River Ehen was always a problem and by 1924 the last pit closed. By the start of World War II, continued subsidence caused the flooding of the area now known as Longlands Lake. Cumbria County Council bought the site in 1980 and have added the footpaths at the start of the walk.

After taking the circular trip around the lake, the route follows the banks of the Ehen before climbing on Wainwright's Coast to Coast walk through forests of pine and spruce. The path finally breaks free on the hilltop of Dent where it marches through wind-bent rushes, mosses and moor grass to a surprise view. Beyond the pale rounded hump of Lank Rigg the skyline is filled with Lakeland peaks, from Grasmoor and High Stile to the mighty crags of Sca Fell and Scafell Pike.

But it's Nannycatch you've come to see, and you only get glimpses from here. Its beauty becomes evident when seen from the steep grassy hill slopes east of the forest. It's hard to believe this little stream has cut such a deep craggy valley, but Nannycatch has a secret: when an ice sheet from the last ice age blocked what is now the Ehen Valley, it was Nannycatch Beck that drained Ennerdale.

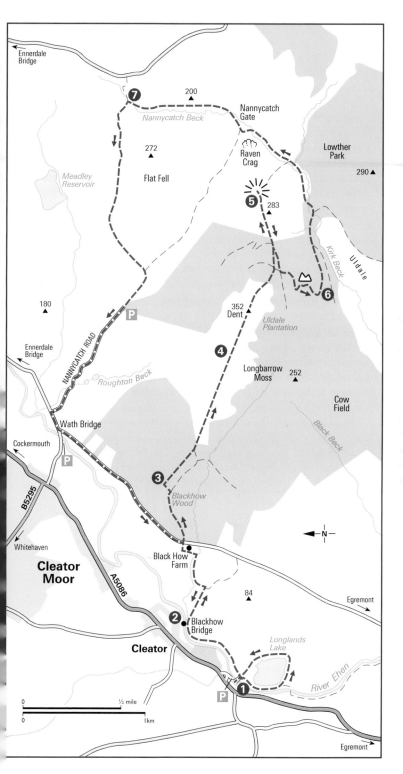

Ennerdale
Bridge

7

Nannycatch Beck

▲ 200

Nannycatch
Gate

Raven
Crag

Lowther
Park

290 ▲

▲ 272

*Meadley
Reservoir*

Flat Fell

5

283
▲

Kirk Beck

Uldale

180
▲

6

Ennerdale
Bridge

352
Dent

*Uldale
Plantation*

NANNYCATCH ROAD

P

4

Longbarrow
Moss

252
▲

Cow
Field

Roughton Beck

Cockermouth

Wath Bridge

P

Black Beck

3

*Blackhow
Wood*

B5295

— N —

Whitehaven

**Cleator
Moor**

Black How
Farm

84
▲

Egremont

A5086

2

Blackhow
Bridge

*Longlands
Lake*

Cleator

1

P

River Ehen

Egremont

0 ———————————— ½ mile
0 ———————————— 1km

Egremont

1. Go over the suspension bridge at the back of the car park and turn right along the circular path around Longlands Lake. Back at the bridge, follow the east bank of the Ehen to Blackhow Bridge.

2. The path quickly swings away from the river. Keep to the enclosed track, following it round several bends. At Black How Farm turn right up the little lane and then cross the road to go through the gate opposite. Follow the forestry track uphill through Blackhow Wood.

3. After half a mile (800m), on drawing level with a gravel area on the right, leave the track for a waymarked path on the left. At another fingerpost, partially hidden by vegetation, turn right to follow a forest ride (or fire-break) up the hill. At the top of the plantation the path follows a fence and then the remains of a wall to the pile of rocks marking the west summit of Dent.

4. Follow the hilltop path over the next top, then through a gate and down a cleared area of Uldale Plantation. At a crossing of paths, go straight over, heading down towards the forest edge, and then left again along a wider track. Watch out for a tall ladder stile on the right – cross this for access to the open fell and that view of Nannycatch.

5. Return to the wide forestry track and turn left. Turn left again at a crossing of ways and descend the stony path that zig-zags steeply down into Uldale.

6. Turn left along the forestry track you meet in Uldale, and cross Kirk Beck. Turn left along another broad track and, almost immediately, go through the gate set back on the left. Recross Kirk Beck and follow the bridleway upstream to Nannycatch Gate. After going through a gate just beyond Raven Crag, ignore the public bridleway on the left and continue alongside Nannycatch Beck.

7. Turn left along the bottom of a dry valley to pick up a well-defined track heading west on the northern flanks of Flat Fell. The path veers left across the grassy slopes to reach a wider gravel path, along which you bear right. Then follow Nannycatch Road down to a T-junction. Turn left here and then left again along a quiet lane on the near side of Wath Bridge. When you get to Black How farm, retrace your steps to the car park, by the side of Longlands Lake.

Where to eat and drink
Like The Gather Café just around the corner, Ennerdale Bridge's Fox and Hounds Inn is owned and run by the local community. Only a short distance from Cleator, it serves a wide range of real ales as well as a hearty menu of good, traditional pub food, including vegetarian dishes.

What to see
You may well see a dipper on Nannycatch Beck. This thrush-sized, plump, dark brown bird with a white throat and breast can be seen flying low or dipping to walk on the stream bed.

While you're there
The Beacon Museum in the picturesque harbour of nearby Whitehaven is an excellent interactive museum where visitors can learn all about the town's history. Experience a shipwreck, relive the Industrial Revolution and even present your own TV weather forecast.

DRAMATIC ST BEES HEAD

DISTANCE/TIME	3.25 miles (5.3km) / 2hrs
ASCENT/GRADIENT	460ft (140m) / ▲ ▲
PATHS	Track, grassy paths and lane, rocks slippery after rain, 7 stiles
LANDSCAPE	Elevated fields, rocky bay, clifftop and open seascapes
SUGGESTED MAP	OS Explorer 303 Whitehaven & Workington
START/FINISH	Grid reference: NX948146
DOG FRIENDLINESS	Good for fit and active dogs under strict control
PARKING	Tarn Flatt Hall Farm by private access road to lighthouse, small fee payable at farmhouse
PUBLIC TOILETS	On seafront at St Bees village

This walk makes a rewarding round of the North Head of St Bees. North Head forms an imposing headland of sandstone looking out across the Irish Sea to the Isle of Man and over the Solway Firth to the hills of Galloway in Scotland. Here you'll find the most spectacular sea cliffs in the northwest of England, home to an important nesting colony of seabirds. The clifftop is largely owned by the Royal Society for the Protection of Birds (RSPB) and this route will be most interesting in the spring and summer months, when the birds are in residence. Even so, the autumnal and winter gales can provide their own attractions on this walk.

A walk on the wild side

When huge breakers roll over Fleswick Bay to smash against the cliffs this walk can become quite dramatic – obviously, some care is needed when things are really rough. At quieter times, Fleswick Bay is a natural sun-trap, and a popular sunbathing and swimming facility for the hardy natives of west Cumbria. The cliffs have also attracted considerable attention from rock climbers. To avoid disturbing nesting birds, a voluntary agreement bars climbing on most of the cliffs from February to July. Bouldering on the rocks below the main cliffs is permitted year-round.

The bay is also a wonderful place to watch birds, as are the clifftops further along the walk. The clifftop viewing areas, built by the RSPB and maintained by a seasonal warden, offer an opportunity to inspect the noisy birdlife nesting on the cliffs below. Many thousands of birds return here each spring to lay their eggs and hatch their chicks before returning to sea where they spend three-quarters of their lives. Most prolific are the guillemots, which resemble dumpy little penguins. Some 5,000 of these birds squeeze precariously onto the narrow open ledges. Razorbills, not so common, can also be seen here along with fulmars, gulls and some 1,600 pairs of kittiwakes. Just beyond the second gate along the top, a pinnacle flake of rock can be seen.

The gap isn't far, though the rift is very deep. Named Cloven Barth on the map, this feature is known locally as Lawson's Leap after a character who thought, fatally, he could make the jump across.

To the lighthouse

The first lighthouse here was built by Thomas Lutwige around 1723. It consisted of a round tower some 30ft (9m) in height, supporting a large metal grate on which coal was burnt. It became the last coal-fired lighthouse in use in Britain, but in 1822, perhaps unsurprisingly, it was destroyed by fire and replaced by an oil-fired lamp in a new tower 56ft (17m) tall. Today the lamp is electric. The lighthouse was automated in 1987 and is now operated remotely from Trinity House's main centre in Harwich. The former keeper's accommodation is now a holiday cottage.

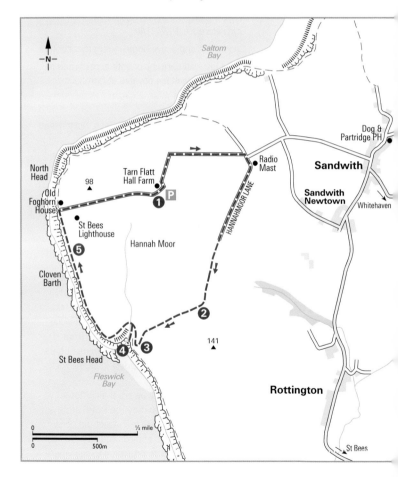

1. From the parking area within the farmyard return to the surfaced road and walk back along to the top of the hill marked by the radio mast. Take the track on the right, Hannahmoor Lane, signed 'Coastal Way Fleswick Bay'. Cross the ladder stile beside the gate and continue along the track, dipping at first and

then rising through more stiles and gates, to climb the shoulder of Hannah Moor. There are grand views east to the Lakeland fells and west across to the Isle of Man.

2. The fifth stile, on the crest of Hannah Moor, has waymark arrows showing the path, which falls diagonally down the next open field. Follow the indicated direction across to the far boundary, then rightwards down the hill. Exit the field by another stile at the bottom and then continue downhill to one further stile.

3. Follow the line of the fence on the right to a kissing gate then descend the path and steps down into a little ravine. At the bottom, just before some steps up to a gate, a little path turns sharply back to the left. Follow this path, crossing and recrossing the stream as necessary, down through the mouth of the canyon to Fleswick Bay.

4. Return up the path and climb the steps to the gate passed earier. Cross the little stream and skirt back left along a slippery shelf of sandstone (needs great care when wet). Another gate leads out onto the open hillside. The steep path, with sections of steps, rises to the cliff top. There are fine views across Fleswick Bay to the cliffs of the South Head. Follow the path beside the fence, which runs close to the cliff edge. At intervals kissing gates in the boundary fence provide access to safe viewing areas.

5. Continue ahead, passing below the main lighthouse, towards the smaller beacon on the cliff edge. Before you reach this you meet a concrete track. Turn right on this and follow it and a continuation lane beyond the main lighthouse to return to Tarn Flatt Hall Farm.

Where to eat and drink
The Dog & Partridge at Sandwith is a 16th-century inn believed to have been a smugglers' haunt. St Bees has several pubs and a café.

What to see
The cliffs of St Bees Head are the only nesting site in England for black guillemots, and they are a relatively common sight around Fleswick Bay in spring and summer. They are identified by the big white wing patch on an otherwise black body and, when out of the water, by their legs and the inside of their beaks (gapes), which are bright scarlet.

While you're there
St Bees village has a beautiful priory church. The original Benedictine foundation was established in the early 12th century and the magnificent Norman west doorway dates from the same period. The priory was supported by landholdings extending far into the fells of the Lake District, including Wasdale and Ennerdale.

NOTES

NOTES

NOTES

Discover quality and friendly B&Bs

RatedTrips.com

AA